Women of Achievement

Nellie Bly

Women *of* Achievement

Abigail Adams

Jane Addams

Susan B. Anthony

Tyra Banks

Clara Barton

Nellie Bly

Julia Child

Hillary Rodham
Clinton

Marie Curie

Ellen DeGeneres

Diana, Princess
of Wales

Amelia Earhart

Tina Fey

Ruth Bader Ginsburg

Joan of Arc

Angelina Jolie

Helen Keller

Madonna

Michelle Obama

Sandra Day O'Connor

Georgia O'Keeffe

Nancy Pelosi

Rachael Ray

Anita Roddick

Eleanor Roosevelt

Martha Stewart

Barbara Walters

Venus and Serena
Williams

Women of Achievement

Nellie Bly

JOURNALIST

John Bankston

CHELSEA HOUSE
An Infobase Learning Company

NELLIE BLY

Chelsea House
An imprint of Infobase Learning
132 West 31st Street
New York NY 10001

Library of Congress Cataloging-in-Publication Data
Bankston, John, 1974–
  Nellie Bly : journalist / by John Bankston.
     p. cm. — (Women of achievement)
  Includes bibliographical references and index.
  ISBN 978-1-60413-908-2
  1. Bly, Nellie, 1864–1922—Juvenile literature. 2. Journalists—United States—Biography—Juvenile literature. 3. Women journalists—United States—Biography—Juvenile literature. I. Title.
  PN4874.C59B35 2011
  070'.92—dc22
  [B]
                              2011000040

Chelsea House books are available at special discounts when purchased in bulk quantities for businesses, associations, institutions, or sales promotions. Please call our Special Sales Department in New York at (212) 967-8800 or (800) 322-8755.

You can find Chelsea House on the World Wide Web at
http://www.infobaselearning.com

Text design by Erik Lindstrom
Cover design by Ben Peterson and Alicia Post
Composition by EJB Publishing Services
Cover printed by Bang Printing, Brainerd, Minn.
Book printed and bound by Bang Printing, Brainerd, Minn.
Date printed: September 2011
Printed in the United States of America

10 9 8 7 6 5 4 3 2 1

This book is printed on acid-free paper.

All links and Web addresses were checked and verified to be correct at the time of publication. Because of the dynamic nature of the Web, some addresses and links may have changed since publication and may no longer be valid.

CONTENTS

Around the World in 72 Days

The decision took more than a year. When it was made, Nellie Bly had less than 48 hours to prepare for the journey of a lifetime.

In 1888, Bly was a reporter for the *New York World*. Like many writers, she was a procrastinator:

> It was my custom to think up ideas on Sunday and lay them before my editor for his approval or disapproval on Monday. But ideas did not come that day and three o'clock in the morning found me weary and with an aching head tossing about in my bed. At last tired and provoked at my slowness in finding a subject, something for the week's work, I

thought fretfully: "I wish I was at the other end of the earth!"[1]

Thus great ideas are born. Fifteen years before, French author Jules Verne had described a man's journey in *Around the World in Eighty Days*. It began with a wager. At his private club, the story's hero listened as fellow members discussed the likelihood of capturing a bank thief. After all, the thief could go anywhere, because "the world is big enough," as one noted.

"It was once," said Phileas Fogg, in a low tone.

A fellow member agreed, adding that "a man can now go round it ten times more quickly than a hundred years ago. And that is why the search for this thief will be more likely to succeed."[2]

The disagreement led to a bet. Could Fogg make it around the world in 80 days? Bly's late-night musings led her to consider a similar expedition. Fogg was a fictional character. Making the trip for real as a single woman required two things: luck and the support of her paper. In 1888, Nellie Bly was short of both.

PHILEAS FOGG

"The idea of a trip around the world pleased me," Nellie Bly later wrote. "If I could do it as quickly as Phileas Fogg did, I should go."[3]

The creation of author Jules Verne, Fogg might never have existed to inspire Bly if Verne had succeeded in the family profession. In 1848, the 20-year-old Verne enrolled in law school with an eye on joining his father's firm. Although he passed his examinations, the future novelist was not very successful as a lawyer. In 1857, shortly after Verne married a widower with two young daughters, Verne's father bought him a seat on the French stock exchange.

Attending law school, practicing law, and in the early morning hours before leaving for work as a stockbroker, Verne wrote. He wrote short stories and plays. None found much of an audience.

He began to write a book after attending meetings at Le Cercle de la Presse Scientifique, a literary club with a scientific bent. He listened as fellow member Félix Tournachon (who was a famous photographer under the name Nadar) described a hot-air balloon he planned to build that would carry a two-story passenger cabin. Inspired by Tournachon's descriptions and two stories from Edgar Allan Poe featuring balloon travel, Verne crafted a nonfiction work incorporating his love of geography and the exploits of recent explorers. In the early 1860s, he hoped his examination of how a piloted balloon could uncover the source of the Nile River would make him a published author.

Unfortunately, one publisher after another rejected it. After the fifteenth rejection, Verne tossed the manuscript into his fireplace. His story was nearly incinerated, but his wife intervened. She pulled it from the flames, insisting he not give up. A few days later, helped by a friend's introduction, Verne met the publisher who changed his life.

Pierre-Jules Hetzel read the book but shook his head as he put it down. Verne prepared for another rejection. Instead, the publisher asked if Verne could turn it into a novel.

Verne did not hesitate. He agreed, signing a 10-year contract for one to two books per year. Some would be serialized in Hetzel's magazine, others published as standalone novels. The books were so successful that the contract was regularly extended. Verne eventually contributed some five dozen books to the "Extraordinary Voyages" series over a period of 60 years (including nine published after his death).

Verne did not wait to see if his first novel would succeed. After telling his wife the good news, he quit his job.

The author was not the first to use science in fiction, but as critic John J. Pierce notes, "Science and technology, which had been peripheral to the travel tale when they appeared at all, were now placed at the center and combined with the elementary appeal of romantic action and adventure."[4] Verne himself realized he had developed a new genre, one that could make him very, very rich if it succeeded.

It succeeded. His first novel, *Five Weeks in a Balloon*, sold well, as did the ones that followed, including *A Journey to the Center of the Earth*, *From the Earth to the Moon*, and *Twenty Thousand Leagues Under the Sea*. Ten years after writing his first novel, Verne published the book that made him rich. *Around the World in Eighty Days* quickly sold more than 500,000 copies, was widely translated, and inspired journalist Nellie Bly. Like Verne's hero, Phileas Fogg, she too encountered numerous obstacles along the way.

THE DREAM

Nellie Bly scarcely slept. Late the next morning she arrived at a steamship company, and after consulting the scheduled departures and arrivals, Bly admitted, "If I had found the elixir of life, I should not have felt better than I did when I conceived a hope that a tour of the world might be made in even less than eighty days."[5]

Her next stop was the *New York World*. She had begun to write for the paper by going undercover at a mental hospital—posing as a patient for nearly two weeks. The abuses she described led to a grand jury investigation.

Bly faced her editor. "Have you any ideas?" John A. Cockerill asked.

She replied, "I want to go around the world in eighty days or less. I think I can beat Phileas Fogg's record. May I try it?"[6]

In his popular novel *Around the World in Eighty Days*, French author Jules Verne created the character of Phileas Fogg, whose heroics circumnavigating the globe inspired journalist Nellie Bly. Stuck for ideas for an article, she pitched a proposal to beat the fictional Fogg's time in traveling around the world.

He was enthusiastic. There was just one problem. A male reporter had already pitched the idea. Bly convinced her editor that a woman making the journey would be more newsworthy.

Armed with her editor's support, the two met with the newspaper's business manager. George W. Turner unearthed more obstacles. Charged with keeping expenses down, the business manager believed her trip would cost twice as much as a man's. Single women needed chaperones, he argued. They also brought so much luggage that they would miss train and ship connections.

Bly was enraged. She did not need a chaperone. She would make do with a single bag.

"Very well," she said. "Start the man, and I'll start the same day for some other newspaper and beat him."[7]

PREPARATIONS

Bly was at work when she was handed a note. Her editor wanted to see her immediately. It was late afternoon. The writer was nervous, certain she was in trouble.

He was writing when she entered his office. She stood there, waiting. Looking up, he asked, "Can you start around the world day after tomorrow?"

"I can start this minute," she answered confidently, despite the rapid beating of her heart. Although she had suggested the trip the year before, she now had less than 48 hours to get ready.[8]

Travel was radically different a century ago. Trips made today by plane were made by either ship or train. What might take 12 hours in the twenty-first century often took a week.

Bly needed a dress she could wear every day for nearly three months. She wanted something reasonably attractive but mainly durable. Bly would travel light and never have to wait for luggage.

Entering the dressmaker's shop, she told him what she needed. A well-constructed, made-to-order dress was challenge enough. Worse, Bly needed it by the close of business. It should have been an impossible request. The reporter was confident it could be done, later writing in her book *Around the World in Seventy-two Days*:

> I always have a comfortable feeling that nothing is impossible if one applies a certain amount of energy in the right direction. When I want things done, which is always at the last moment, and I am met with such an answer: "It's too late. I hardly think it

DID YOU KNOW?

The following is how Nellie Bly described what went into her bag:

> Two traveling caps, three veils, a pair of slippers, a complete outfit of toilet articles, ink-stand, pens, pencils, and copy-paper, pins, needles and thread, a dressing gown, a tennis blazer, a small flask and a drinking cup, several complete changes of underwear, a liberal supply of handkerchiefs and fresh ruchings [lace ruffles] and most bulky and uncompromising of all, a jar of cold cream to keep my face from chapping in the varied climates I should encounter.
>
> That jar of cold cream was the bane of my existence. It seemed to take up more room than everything else in the bag and was always getting into just the place that would keep me from closing the satchel.*

* Nellie Bly, *Around the World in Seventy-two Days*. New York: Pictorial Weeklies, 1890, p. 1. http://digital.library.upenn.edu/women/bly/world/world.html.

can be done," I simply say: "Nonsense! If you want to do it, you can do it. The question is, do you want to do it?" I have never met the man or woman yet who was not aroused by that answer into doing their very best.[9]

The dressmaker finished the dress on time. Back at home the reporter selected a single piece of luggage. She needed to pack all she would require for the next 10 weeks. It was a daunting task, but she managed.

The next day she purchased her tickets from New York to London onboard the steamship *Augusta Victoria*. Although Bly could have purchased tickets for the entire journey, she decided to wait. If she missed a connection or found a faster way, she would have more options. She acquired a passport—number 247—and received £200 in English gold and Bank of England notes. She placed the notes in a chamois bag, which she tied around her neck; the gold went in a pocket. She also carried some U.S. currency to discover where in the world it would be accepted. With everything prepared, she went to bed for a night of restless sleep.

BON VOYAGE

Bly was not a morning person. The ship set sail at 9:40 A.M. In the wee hours of the night, she worried that she would oversleep. "Those who think that night is the best part of the day and that morning was made for sleep, know how uncomfortable they feel when for some reason they have to get up with—well, with the milkman," she later recalled.

I thought lazily that if some of these good people who spend so much time in trying to invent flying machines would only devote a little of the same energy towards promoting a system by which boats

One bag in hand (rather than the many pieces of luggage her
newspaper's business manager thought a woman would need),
Nellie Bly was ready to travel around the world. She had proposed the trip in 1888; when her editor gave his approval a year
later, Bly had only 48 hours to get ready.

and trains would always make their start at noon or afterwards, they would be of greater assistance to suffering humanity.[10]

Bly made the ship. "The *World* today undertakes the task of turning a dream into a reality," the paper promised on November 14, 1889—the day she left the United States. "Nellie Bly, so well known to millions who have read of her doings, as told by her captivating pen, will set out as a female Phileas Fogg." Besides publishing her itinerary and promising updates (as up-to-date as a paper could be in the telegraph age), the *World* held a sweepstakes to increase reader interest during her long journey.[11]

Boarding the *Augusta Victoria*, Bly was accompanied by a few friends. She later wrote:

> "Don't worry," I said encouragingly, as I was unable to speak that dreadful word, "goodbye;" "only think of me as having a vacation and the most enjoyable time in my life." Then to encourage myself, I thought, as I was on my way to the ship: "It's only a matter of 28,000 miles, and seventy-five days and four hours, until I shall be back again."

Yet as her friends left the ship and her ship left the harbor for the open waters of the Atlantic Ocean, Bly's confidence waned. "I am off," she thought, "and shall I ever get back?"[12]

It was a question asked across the country. Bly's name would soon be known across the world. She was, as biographer Brooke Kroeger points out,

> one of the late nineteenth century's most rousing characters. In the 1880s she pioneered the development of "detective" or "stunt" reporting, the

acknowledged forerunner of full-scale investigative journalism. While still in her twenties, the example of her fearless success helped open the profession to coming generations of women journalists clamoring to write hard news.[13]

Although Bly dreamed of being a writer, as a teenager it seemed an impossible dream. She had dropped out of high school because her family could not afford the tuition. At 20, she was helping her mother run a boardinghouse when she first contacted a newspaper. A columnist had said women should not work, that they should stay home and raise children. Bly disagreed. Her response not only changed her life; it began a career that changed the lives of thousands—both the downtrodden she reported on and the female writers inspired by her words.

A Girl
Named Pink

Taking place in the rough country of Spotsylvania County not far from the nation's capital, the Battle of the Wilderness altered neither borders nor the war. Yet May 5, 1864, was etched upon the tombstones of the thousands who fought and died during the Civil War conflict in Central Virginia's nearly impenetrable woods.

Overnight, a brush fire swept across the conflict's no-man's-land, an area between the two opposing armies controlled by neither. The blaze extinguished the lives of the wounded, their screams echoing across the valley. The next day, acrid smoke from rifles and the fire wafted away. More than 25,000 soldiers had been killed or wounded.

For the Confederates, the battle was a victory. It was one of many, but Confederate successes were eventually rendered meaningless by the Union's superior numbers and armaments.

Three hundred miles (480 kilometers) north, a girl who became famous for fighting battles with longer-lasting consequences but fewer casualties was born. Her mother, Mary Jane Cochran, was the second wife of Judge Michael Cochran. He had fathered 10 children with a previous wife and two sons, five-year-old Albert Paul and three-year-old Charles Metzger, with his second. When Elizabeth Jane Cochran was born that May day, she enjoyed a favored position as the couple's first daughter.

Despite her future fame, the birth date of the girl later known as Nellie Bly is still disputed. She came of age in an era when even official documents were unreliable.

Acquiring a passport in the late 1880s, she gave her birth date as "May 5, 1867. Age 22," notes biographer Brooke Kroeger in her book, *Nellie Bly: Daredevil, Reporter, Feminist.* "That the very youthful-looking Bly elected to declare for herself a new birth date . . . is of little consequence," for Bly "looked even younger than twenty-two and had a great deal invested in being that plucky girl reporter. What possible difference could it make to her government if she were born in 1864 or 1867? Her birth was never registered, and anyway, who would check?"[1]

Today *Contemporary Authors Online* lists her date of birth as May 5, 1866, while the *Dictionary of American Biography* uses Bly's passport date. Although the *Encyclopedia of World Biography* lists May 5, 1864, the disagreement among generally reliable sources is something Kroeger argued against explaining, "I located Bly's baptismal record which puts the confusion Bly had caused on the question of her birth date to permanent rest."[2]

That baptism, conducted at the local Methodist Episcopal church, was one of the few occasions when Elizabeth Jane's proper name was used. Even then, she attracted attention. Young girls in the 1860s usually wore muted shades of gray and brown. Not Elizabeth Jane—before she could even walk, her mother dressed her in the bright, happy color that earned the toddler her first nickname: Pink.

"Pink" Cochran's early childhood was spent in the town named after her father. Michael Cochran had transformed the economy of Pitt's Mills, modernizing its four-story gristmill, operating a general store, and earning a small fortune in real estate speculation. Five years after his 1850 election as associate justice for Armstrong County, the town was renamed in his honor.

Despite the accolade, when Pink was five, the family relocated to Michael Cochran's hometown. In Apollo, Pennsylvania, they settled into a 10,000-square-foot (930-square-meter) mansion, surrounded by several acres of pristine property. The new home provided enough space for the family's cow, horse, and two dogs. It also offered more than enough room for Pink, who, despite her girlish attire and two older half-sisters at home, did all she could to keep up with her brothers.

It was an idyllic life. Unfortunately, it did not last long.

TRAGIC CHANGES

As travel modernized in the nineteenth century, Apollo benefited from its proximity to Pittsburgh. Located 35 miles (56 kilometers) from the city in Armstrong County, it was in a region where coal mining was the primary industry. When the Cochrans moved into their new house, the town boasted 700 residents; in 40 years there would be more than 3,000.

The life Pink enjoyed as the favored child of a successful father ended in the summer of 1870. After a short illness, Judge Cochran died on July 18.

Despite his legal background, he died without a will. Less than two months later, Robert Scott Cochran (the judge's first-born son) went to court to begin the process of dividing the estate. With so many children entitled to a share of his wealth, most of his property was sold—including the house in Apollo.

Mary Jane was entitled to "the widow's third." One-third of the estate was held in a trust from which she earned interest. Combined with the money she received for the care of the minor children, she received about $500 per year. It was a tidy sum in the 1870s but would not come close to supporting her lifestyle.

Mary Jane Cochran purchased a small, two-story wood-frame home in Apollo for $200. In October, she and her children moved into the cramped, five-room home. Young Pink suffered considerably. She began to write, in part to escape her altered circumstances.

"She wrote love and fairy stories by the score," Bly recalled, describing herself as a young girl. "For whole hours at night she lay in bed unable to go to sleep because of the tirelessness of her imagination, weaving tales and creating heroes and heroines simply for her own delight or gratification of the young companions to whom she would relate them."[3]

When not imagining better worlds, she was, in the words of one peer, "rather wild." By the time she was seven, she began to attend school with her siblings. After walking the short distance, they entered a two-story building with a room for high school students and another for the primary

DID YOU KNOW?

Apollo, Pa., is a palindrome—it is spelled the same backward or forward.

grades. A single teacher taught each section, overseeing dozens of students. They were expected to be well-behaved, notes biographer Kroeger, with a swift response for those who were not. "For punishment there were willow rods, usually cracked off trees up the ravine in Owens' Woods." Young Pink evidently felt their sting more than once.[4]

Pink's difficulties at school, however, were nothing compared to what she would soon face at home. Her mother was about to remarry.

A VIOLENT HOME

"[J.J.] Ford has been generally drunk since they were married," Pink remembered. "When drunk he is very cross and cross when sober. . . . The first time I seen Ford take hold of mother in an angry manner, he attempted to choke her."[5]

When Mary Jane Cochran married Ford in January 1873, he brought to the union bad debts, a spotty employment history, and apparent alcoholism. What Pink endured during the next half-dozen years profoundly influenced her later choices.

A year after the wedding, Mary Jane helped her new husband open a grocery store with her son Albert. There she made and sold ice cream. The business struggled, hurt in part by the regular arguments between Albert and Ford. After a year, their partnership dissolved when Ford pulled a gun and threatened to kill Albert. On January 1, 1878, Ford again pointed a gun at a family member.

Upset that Mary Jane had defied his orders and attended the Methodist Episcopal church's New Year's Eve celebration, he laid in wait for her return. When she arrived home, he pointed a pistol at her. He promised to kill her; only the intervention of two townspeople and Albert saved her life.

Mary Jane moved out for several days, but the couple soon reconciled. In spite of his behavior, forgiving such abuse was common. Despite his meager contributions to the family, Mary Jane seemed unconvinced that she could make it without him.

Nine months later, an argument on September 30 continued into the next day. Ford punched holes in the walls, tossed clean laundry into the backyard, and poured dirty water onto it. At the dinner table, he threw his coffee onto the floor and hurled a bone at his wife. After she threw it back, he drew his pistol. This time Pink helped Albert prevent Ford from murdering their mother.

On October 14, 1878, Mary Jane Cochran filed for divorce. Pink was 14. Divorce was rare in the 1870s. With a population of 40,000, Armstrong County had 15 divorces in 1878. Including Cochran's, there were only five in which the wife was the one suing.

In the twenty-first century, divorces are often no-fault. *Black's Law Dictionary* defines this as "a divorce in which the parties are not required to prove fault or grounds beyond a

THE VICTORIANS

Although the Victorian Era is associated with Great Britain and the reign of Queen Victoria from 1837 to 1901, its values reached the United States. It was a time of great contradictions. On the one hand, the era featured a strict moral code and intolerance for deviations from what was considered acceptable conduct. Yet the period also saw an increase in child labor and urban crime. It was marked by numerous inventions along with the notion that science could solve human problems. Both in the United States and England, men and women were expected to dress conservatively and maintain traditional gender roles.

showing of the irretrievable breakdown of the marriage or irreconcilable differences."[6]

In the nineteenth century, divorce required grounds—generally either abuse or adultery—and witnesses to validate those claims. Pink had to swear before a judge that her stepfather was abusive.

It was not easy. She divulged private details about her family and repeated under oath the profanity Ford directed toward her mother. Although it was necessary to validate her mother's charge against Ford of "cruel and barbarous treatment," testifying meant using words inappropriate for a young lady in Victorian times.

By the time the divorce was granted in the summer of 1879, Pink was devising the best strategy to earn a living. She never wanted to rely on an unreliable man or count on her family. In the beginning, she had to do both.

LACK OF TRUST

The future Nellie Bly was an early master of reinvention. It was a common quality in her young country. Across the Atlantic, family land and the trades of Europe's workers were passed down to each generation. In England's former colony, young adults pursued dreams different from those of their parents. Dreamers were driven by land rushes, gold rushes, and the ever-expanding borders.

The Indiana Normal School in Indiana, Pennsylvania, was 15 miles (24 kilometers) to the east of Apollo. Opened in May 1875, its single building housed all the classes and a model school for students to practice teaching. A coeducational facility when most schools educated men and women separately, the Indiana Normal School accepted boys and girls over the age of 14 who wanted to study business or education.

Pink felt like a pioneer. On her application to the school, she buried her childhood nickname and added an "e" to her last name. "Elizabeth J. Cochrane" looked sophisticated,

Colonel Samuel Jackson, who administered the estate of Michael Cochran, told young Elizabeth Jane Cochran (Nellie Bly's given name) that there was enough money for her to attend the Indiana Normal School for three years. The money ran out before she even finished a semester.

she believed. Other family members followed her lead; even her mother adopted the vowel.

To become a teacher, she would have to study for three years. The total cost approached $500. Although her mother supported the decision, she did not have the money. Elizabeth visited Colonel Samuel Jackson, the administrator of her father's estate.

Besides making regular payments to Mary Jane Cochrane from the "widow's third," Jackson managed the minor children's investments and paid their medical and educational expenses. He assured Elizabeth that there would be enough money for her to complete three years at the Indiana Normal School.

Cochrane began to attend classes on September 8, 1879. She joined nearly 300 students almost equally divided between boys and girls. Jackson signed the enrollment form as her guardian.

She enjoyed her studies but was still an unpolished writer. "I teach in model school," she wrote to Albert. "Ain't I a young teacher. Be a good boy and remember me in your prayers."[7]

Her excitement soon ended. Jackson had lied. Before the first semester concluded, he told Elizabeth the truth. There was not enough money for her tuition.

There were no scholarships, no financial aid, and no money offered from family members. Later, she claimed to have attended for two years, dropping out because of a heart condition. Instead, she did not even take her finals. By early 1880, a dejected Elizabeth moved home, with neither education nor prospects.

Lonely
Orphan Girl

Pittsburgh is an industrial city. In the 1880s, its factories operated around the clock, producing the steel, refining the oil, and manufacturing the goods desired by a newly industrializing nation. Along its shoreline where the Allegheny and Monongahela Rivers joined to form the Ohio, manufacturers dumped pollutants into the water. Across the region, smokestacks spewed chemicals into the air. It was a place that valued work above all else, where literature and the arts were seen as distractions, a city described by resident J. Ernest Wright as the "blackest, dirtiest, grimmest city in the United States."[1]

Elizabeth Jane Cochran was born in Cochran Mills, but Pittsburgh, Pennsylvania, was Nellie Bly's birthplace. Just a few miles north, Allegheny City grew in tandem with its larger neighbor. When the Cochranes settled there in the early 1880s, it was home to nearly 80,000 residents, while Pittsburgh boasted more than 155,000.

Albert, Elizabeth Cochrane's oldest full brother, was in his early 20s when he arrived. A few months later, his mother, Mary Jane Cochrane, rented a home at 50 Miller Street in the industrialized Manchester neighborhood. She was joined in the tiny row house by Albert and Elizabeth, 18-year-old Charles, 14-year-old Catherine, and 10-year-old Harry. In 1881, Charles married and moved out.

Mary Jane Cochrane would not sell her home in Apollo for another decade. Until her first-born daughter became successful, she lived in a series of modest rented row houses, mostly in working-class neighborhoods. By the time she arrived on Arch Street five years after moving to Allegheny City, she was taking in boarders. Thus she could afford a decent home in a respectable neighborhood. Her tenants were generally single men employed by the Baltimore and Ohio Railroad. A railroad sleeping car conductor may have met the youngest daughter while paying her mother rent. He married Catherine soon after her sixteenth birthday.

Elizabeth Jane was in her late teens when two of her siblings got married. She was not interested.

In the 1880s, a woman her age was considered ideal for marriage. In 10 years, she would be considered an "old maid." A witness to two of her mother's marriages, Elizabeth Jane Cochrane was scared of both widowhood and divorce. To her there was no such thing as a happy marriage.

She did not look for a husband. She looked for a job. As a divorced widow, her mother still needed help from men—even if they were her tenants. Although Elizabeth Jane refused to rely on a man for support, what she did for money during the four years after leaving the Indiana Normal School is unclear.

Back in the late nineteenth century, as one resident said, Pittsburgh was the "blackest, dirtiest, grimmest city in the United States"—as this illustration from 1882 shows. In the early 1880s, Elizabeth Jane and her family moved from the countryside to Allegheny City, industrial Pittsburgh's neighbor.

A decade later, brief biographical sketches of her appeared. Most claimed she spent the time reading, writing, and developing her equestrian skills. The relaxed lifestyle of literature and horseback riding seems unlikely given her meager financial circumstances. With the modest trust depleted and her mother relying on boarders, there was probably little time for leisure activities.

Her life from 1880 to 1885 was most likely devoted to a series of unpleasant, menial jobs with little opportunity for advancement. "There are indications she tried her hand at tutoring, nannying, maybe even housekeeping, while her brothers, with less education, were able to land acceptable positions," biographer Brooke Kroeger writes.[2]

She exaggerated her education. It made little difference. Then she read the column that changed her life.

THE QUIET OBSERVER

Pittsburgh, like most growing cities in the late 1800s, supported a number of daily newspapers. Without radio or television, newspapers were the primary source of information for citizens. Most papers reflected the beliefs and biases of their owners, not just in the opinion sections but on the front page. The *Pittsburg Dispatch* (as the paper spelled the city's name back then) offered both an independent Republican point of view and the city's most popular columnist.

Columnists were often celebrities, and Erasmus Wilson was the most celebrated in Pittsburgh. As the "Quiet Observer," he sought to "pose the same old topics so they may be seen at different angles than those from which they are usually viewed. This gives them a new aspect without rendering them strange or unfamiliar."[3]

Wilson explored controversial topics by offering conventional opinions in a confrontational manner. In the later nineteenth century, the role of women in the workplace was one of these topics. It was a subject that would be debated for more than a century afterward.

In the early twenty-first century, women make up 59.5 percent of the labor force, with some 121 million women over the age of 16 working or looking for work. In the 1880s, it was less than 20 percent. Today 55 percent of mothers work outside of the home. Although most with children rely on day care, nannies, and schools, increasingly "stay-at-home" husbands take care of their offspring while their wives work.

In 1880, the ranks of traditionally female jobs like teaching and nursing were filled by single women. If they married, they usually quit. Despite this reality, Wilson believed that working women threatened the institution of marriage, and by extension the family.

In a column he entitled "Women's Sphere," he criticized "restless dissatisfied females who think they are out of their spheres and go around giving everybody fits for not helping them to find them." Instead of searching for their ideal place in the world (or the best job), they should labor to ensure that their "home [was] a little paradise, herself playing the part of angel."[4]

A father wrote to Wilson, complaining about his teenage and twenty-something daughters: "I have five of them on hand, and am at a loss how to get them off or what use to make of them." Wilson did not advise the father; he advised society. "Girls say they would sooner die than live to be old maids and young men claim they cannot afford to marry until they get rich because wives are such expensive luxuries." In another column he criticized "women who . . . rush into the breaches under the guise of defending their rights," when he saw it as "an effort to wrest from man certain [rights] bequeathed him by heaven." To him women who fought for those rights were "disgusting to womanly women and manly men. . . . There is no greater abnormity than a woman in breeches [trousers] unless it is a man in petticoats."[5]

Wilson wrote in conservative times, and his beliefs reflected the era. Yet they still stirred outrage. Wrote one female reader:

> I am old enough to vote, if selfish man would give me a chance, yet not so old but what I may reasonably hope to see the day when women will march to the polls in a solid phalanx and assert their rights. I

have had plenty of opportunities to marry, and, if so disposed, can go out now and pick up any one of a half-dozen good men and be at the head of a domestic establishment, but I don't want to.[6]

One of the newspaper's regular readers was a young woman who imagined Wilson as a short "grey-haired, sharp-nosed sour-visaged [faced] chap who could look clean through you." The Quiet Observer was actually a tall, country gentleman who struck most who met him as resembling nothing more than a kindly uncle. Yet reading the series of columns he wrote in January 1885, the woman was outraged. Her fury increased with each dispatch, reaching a boiling point after his "man in petticoats" comment. As she grew increasingly angry with Q.O.'s columns, Elizabeth Cochrane could not have imagined that the man who wrote them would soon become one of her most ardent supporters.[7]

FOUR STORIES TO THE TOP

Enraged by what she had read, Elizabeth Cochrane wrote a letter to the *Dispatch*. The disappointments and struggles she had endured were poured passionately onto the over-sized sheet of cheap paper.

She only had to look at her mother's life, and her own, to see inaccuracies in Wilson's point of view. The choice about whether to work was not a choice for many women. It was a necessity.

Some women did not have the option of marriage—even one without "luxuries."

Even if they did, so what—Cochrane did not think women should be forced to rely on a man, nor should they be forced to labor for years in menial jobs. Men could start at companies as clerks and work their way up to managing the operation. Women were "just as smart," she argued, "and a great deal quicker to learn; why then can they not do the same?"[8]

Cochrane did not feel comfortable revealing her name or address. Instead, she signed the letter, "Lonely Orphan Girl."

When the letter reached the office of the *Pittsburg Dispatch*, managing editor George Madden was intrigued. He handed the large sheet of paper to Wilson. "She isn't much for style," he told The Quiet Observer, "but what she has to say she says it right out regardless of paragraphs or punctuation. She knocks it off, and it is just right, too."[9]

What Madden saw in the raw prose of a woman barely out of her teens was the sharp observational skills and honest reporting of a veteran journalist. He did not feel her letter suitable for publication, but he wanted to get in touch with her. Unfortunately, he had no easy way to contact the "Lonely Orphan Girl."

Wilson suggested that Madden put an ad in the letters to the editor section. On Saturday, January 17, 1885, this plea appeared in "Mail Pouch": "If the writer of the communication signed 'Lonely Orphan Girl' will send her name and address to this office, merely as a guarantee of good faith, she will confer a favor and receive the information she desires."[10]

Elizabeth Cochrane opened the *Pittsburg Dispatch* hoping to see her letter in print. Instead, she saw the request for her to write another letter. It was exactly the opportunity she dreamed of. She was not going to wait for the mailman. She did not even wait for the workweek to begin. Early the next day, she set out for the paper's offices.

There was no elevator. Instead, Cochrane ascended four flights of stairs. Dressed in an outer wrap of Russian black silk and a fur hat, she was perspiring by the time she reached the top despite the season.

Cochrane was lucky. Although it was a Sunday, the paper's offices were bustling. In a whisper, nearly hyperventilating, she asked a clerk where she might find the editor. Wilson was nearby, watching as the office boy pointed to Madden. "The girl's countenance [face] brightened, and she smiled for the first time, showing a beautiful set of teeth.

FEMALE JOURNALISTS

In the late 1800s, journalism was an overwhelmingly male profession. Generally fond of cigars, with more street smarts than book smarts, the men Elizabeth "Nellie Bly" Cochrane met were not very accepting of female journalists. That attitude evolved. Writing about female reporters in the *Journalist*, Thomas F. Anderson explained, "She is an indispensible reality, joyfully hailed as the delivery of mankind from the horrors of high weddings, dry goods openings, woman suffrage conventions and fashionable balls."*

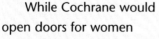

Nellie Bly was not the only woman journalist who investigated hard news in the late 1800s and early 1900s. Ida Tarbell (*above*) wrote a 19-part series, "The History of the Standard Oil Company," that exposed the company's shady business practices.

While Cochrane would open doors for women who wanted to do more than society reporting, she was by no means the first female reporter. Maria "Middy" Morgan worked as a livestock reporter for the *New York Times* in the

"'Oh is it?' she asked. 'I expected to see an old cross man.'"[11]

Madden overheard but was not offended. He was the opposite of her expectations—young and energetic with

late eighteenth century, while competitors like Nell Nelson and Elizabeth Bisland worked on many of the same stories as Bly.

Bessie Bramble, the pseudonym of banker Charles Isaac Wade's wife, also wrote for the *Pittsburg Dispatch* in the 1880s. Despite a privileged background, she covered many of the same issues Bly did—divorce, working women—and in 1892 she was the first woman to join the Pittsburgh Press Club.

The only female graduate of Allegheny College in 1880, Ida Tarbell went on to write for a number of magazines. Her 19-part series "The History of the Standard Oil Company," published from November 1902 to October 1904, exposed a number of questionable business practices by the company. Tarball was part of a new generation of investigative journalists that President Theodore Roosevelt called "muckrakers."

In the 1840s, essayist Margaret Fuller actually covered the Blackwell's Island asylum. Her work, however, did not reveal as much as Bly's would decades later.

Writing as Jennie June, Jane Cunningham was the first woman to hold a regular salaried position at a major U.S. newspaper. Beginning in the mid-1850s, her articles on topics such as fashion and entertainment were focused on attracting women readers but actually interested both genders. As an editor she is credited with beginning the so-called women's pages.

---

* Brooke Kroeger, *Nellie Bly: Daredevil, Reporter, Feminist.* New York: Random House, 1994, p. 193.

ambitious plans for the paper. Having worked his way up from menial jobs to stints as a reporter at a number of rival papers, he championed diverse points of view and modern reporting in his new position as managing editor. When he approached the young woman, her anxiety lessened.

Cochrane expected "a great big man with a bushy beard who would look over the top of his specs and snap, 'What do you want?'" Madden, she recalled, was a "mild-mannered, pleasant faced boy," while Wilson was "a great big good-natured fellow who wouldn't even kill the nasty roaches that crawled over his desk. There wasn't an old cross man about the place."[12]

Before meeting Cochrane, Madden had hoped the "Lonely Orphan Girl" would write for the *Dispatch*. After a brief conversation, he believed she was up to the challenge. Cochrane left the paper with an assignment and the possibility for more. Soon she would earn a new name as well: Nellie Bly.

Nellie Bly
Is Born!

There are more cooks, chambermaids and washerwomen than can find employment. In fact, all places that are filled by women are overrun, and still there are idle girls, some that have aged parents depending on them. We cannot let them starve. Can they that have full and plenty of this world's goods realize what it is to be a poor working woman, abiding in one or two bare rooms, without fire enough to keep warm, while her threadbare clothes refuse to protect her from the wind and cold, and denying herself necessary food that her little ones may not go hungry; fearing the landlord's frown and threat to cast her out and sell what little she has, begging for employment of any kind that she may earn enough to pay for the bare rooms she calls home, no one to speak kindly to or encourage her, nothing to make life worth living?[1]

—From "The Girl Puzzle" by Nellie Bly, January 25, 1885

"The Girl Puzzle" was Nellie Bly's first published piece, appearing just one week after her meeting with the *Pittsburg Dispatch*'s managing editor. George Madden ran it on page 11 of the paper's new Sunday edition. Such an achievement for a 20-year-old with little education and no experience in journalism was impressive, regardless of gender.

On her first published piece, Cochrane's byline (the writer's name that appears with the article) was "Orphan Girl." For the work she received $5 and another assignment. Pleased with her first effort, Madden asked if she had suggestions for the next one. It took her only a moment to answer. She wanted to write about divorce.

Reporters are expected to uncover information from every side and present an unbiased article. Columnists often use facts to inform their writing—frequently using journalistic techniques—but they use those facts to support a point of view. Even in the early stages of her career, Cochrane blended the jobs of reporter and columnist. The articles she wrote might be similar in placement and subject matter to others in the paper, but they included her point of view. And no matter the topic, she was a part of the story.

While her first article drew from her experiences as a young woman, the second was informed by the traumas she endured as a teenager. Cochrane believed that, if couples entered matrimony fully informed, there would be fewer divorces. She must have considered her mother's marriage to J.J. Ford when she wrote, "Let the young girl know that her intended is cross, surly, uncouth; let the young man know that his affirmed is anything that is direct opposite to an angel. Tell all their faults, then if they marry so be it, they cannot say, 'I did not know,' but the world can say, 'I told you so.'"[2]

Despite applauding Pennsylvania Governor Robert E. Pattison's recent efforts to reform the state's divorce laws, she was more enthusiastic about the stricter regulations found in the German state of Bavaria. There, couples were unable to marry if either of them received the nineteenth-century equivalent of welfare—"public charity"—within the last three years. They were also forbidden to marry if they owed taxes or if their laziness, bad habits, or poverty were likely to create an unhappy home and lead to divorce. Cochrane's article also included what was most likely a not-so-subtle shot at her older brother, Albert:

> A young man drawing a comfortable income has a widowed mother, who has doubtless worked hard to give him a start in life, and helpless sisters. He lets his aged mother work, and allows his sisters to support themselves where and how they will, never has five cents or a kind word to give at home, dresses in the height of fashion, has every enjoyment, gives his lady friends costly presents, takes them to places of amusement, tries to keep it a secret that his mothers and sisters work. If the fact becomes known, he will assert positively that it is against his most urgent desire. Will he make a good husband, do you think?[3]

"Mad Marriages" earned the fledgling writer numerous letters. It also earned a job offer from Madden. He would pay her $5 a week and give her a new name.

BIRTH OF NELLIE BLY

Editor George Madden faced a deadline. The printing press would not wait. Articles and columns had been edited

After her first two articles for the *Pittsburg Dispatch* were published, 20-year-old Elizabeth Cochrane received a full-time job offer, paying her $5 a week. She also received the name by which the world would come to know her—Nellie Bly.

and typeset, the illustrations were inserted, the advertising properly placed. The February 1 edition of the *Pittsburg Dispatch* was almost ready. Madden still had a problem. What was he going to call Elizabeth Cochrane?

Cochrane needed a proper byline for her piece on divorce. Today newspaper articles are generally written under a reporter's legal name. In the 1880s, female reporters used pseudonyms. The made-up names were considered a good way to protect the reputation of women engaged in the disreputable male profession of journalism.

Madden looked around. Did anyone in the newsroom have a suggestion? Someone shouted out, "Nelly Bly."

Authored 35 years before by the famous Pittsburgh songwriter Stephen Collins Foster, the song "Nelly Bly" was inspired by his friend Henry Woods's servant. Bly's mother had been a slave. Foster, still remembered for his song "Oh! Susanna," gained popularity with pre-Civil War minstrelsy. A popular entertainment, it relied on white singers in blackface and stereotypical dialects. Thus the song Nelly Bly features the lyrics: "Nelly Bly hab a voice like a turtle dove, I hears it in de meadow and I hears it in de grove. Nelly Bly has a heart warm as a cup ob tea, and bigger dan de sweet potato down in Tennessee."[4]

Madden felt it an appropriate pseudonym for a woman writing about the bonds her gender was enslaved by, even if the bonds were figurative and the "slavery" not literal. Considering other options, he was interrupted by the cry of "Copy!" Out of time, he scrawled the name across the piece—misspelling the song title—and handed it to the copyboy, sending it on its journey to becoming a published article. Nellie Bly was born when Cochrane was 20 years old.

By the time of Bly's "birth," Elizabeth Cochrane was busy working on her next assignment—writing about the women who labored in local factories. Her staff job and the

$5 a week it provided was roughly what they earned, and not much more than she had made in more menial professions. Being paid a salary to be a writer, however, made up for that.

FACTORY "GIRLS"

Factories employing the women Bly interviewed were radically different from those 30 years later. In the early 1900s, automobile pioneer Henry Ford's development of the assembly line changed the way factory workers worked. Relying on a series of conveyor belts, the system brought the parts of a car to be assembled to the worker. In the 1880s, workers went to the parts, usually laboring together around a table.

The assembly line drastically increased worker productivity—each worker produced more each hour. More products meant more profits and enabled employers to pay more. Automobile manufacturing plants usually employed men; the less productive factory workers (who earned less) were often women.

Instead of being paid a wage of so much per hour or per week, the women Bly met were paid by the piece. Each completed piece earned the worker a fraction of a cent; it took hundreds, even thousands of pieces a week to make enough to live on. Those who could not complete a decent number quickly quit.

A few years later in an article about New York women employed by a box factory, Bly quoted one who admitted, "Girls do not get paid half enough at work. Box factories are no worse than other places. I do not know anything a girl can do where by hard work she can earn more than six dollars a week. A girl cannot dress and pay her boarding on that."[5]

In the same article, another woman conceded that she had worked at a box factory "for eleven years, and I can't say

THE INDUSTRIAL REVOLUTION

Although it began in England, the Industrial Revolution soon spread to its former colony. In the early 1800s, most goods were handcrafted in small, usually home-based businesses. Scottish engineer James Watt's improvement of the steam engine in 1785 helped power larger operations, while with the interchangeable parts Eli Whitney developed for a 1798 military contract, products could be assembled many miles from where their individual components were produced. These developments led to factories where large quantities of goods were produced by low-skilled labor (instead of by craftspeople). Since people had to keep up with machines, it also meant work became fast-paced and tedious.

In 1791, founding father Alexander Hamilton predicted that men would remain on farms while women would work in manufacturing facilities. Writing in his *Report on Manufactures*, Hamilton explained that factories allowed "the employment of persons who would otherwise be idle (and in many cases a burden on the community). . . . It is worthy of particular remark, that in general, women and children are rendered more useful, and the latter more early useful by manufacturing establishments, than they otherwise would be."*

By 1860, approximately 14 percent of women over 16 worked for wages while 20 percent of manufacturing employees were women. One-quarter of those were under the age of 16.

---

* Rosalyn Baxandall and Linda Gordon, eds. *America's Working Women: A Documentary History, 1600 to the Present*. New York: W.W. Norton, 1995, p. 22.

it has ever given me a living. . . . I have to work very hard and without ceasing to be able to make two hundred boxes a day, which earns me $1. . . . Cheap labor, isn't it?"[6]

While Bly's later reporting focused on working conditions, the *Pittsburg Dispatch* articles took a different approach. They were more gossipy, looking at how the women lived when they were not working. Madden suggested that she go to the factories to discover what the conditions there were like. Accompanied by an illustrator, Bly embarked on her first investigative series—a total of eight articles running on consecutive Sundays.

Her early work lacked a veteran reporter's skepticism. She believed her subjects and did not investigate their claims.

She quoted one employee about the dreadful condition of the factory she once worked at, but neither named the business nor attempted to see it. She described the factories she visited as clean, safe, and decent places to work. While she reported the practice of employing girls as young as eight, she took the word of the foreman who claimed, "It is not their custom to take such young girls, but mothers come with tears in their eyes and beg work for them to help along at home." Bly's piece asserted, "This is undoubtedly an act of kindness and charity, and if this rule was lived up to by all the employers of child labor in [Pittsburgh and Allegheny City], many a home would be cheered and to many worthy ones extended a helping hand."[7]

While she was still raw as a writer and a journalist, as an interviewer she excelled. She put her subjects at ease, instinctively asking questions that yielded interesting quotations.

One of the factory women admitted to "catching a mash"—meeting a man at a bar, drinking, and going home with him. Bly asked why the woman risked her reputation. "I don't think I ever had one to risk," her subject laughed.

Women garment workers are shown toiling in the dressmaking department of a factory in the late nineteenth century. In one of her first assignments, Nellie Bly wrote an eight-part series about female factory workers. While Bly did not yet have the skepticism of a veteran reporter, her interviewing skills were evident right away.

"I work hard all day, week after week, for a mere pittance. I go home at night tired of labor and longing for something new, anything good or bad to break the monotony of my existence."[8]

Sentence construction, grammar, and writing concise copy were teachable skills. Madden and Wilson worked hard to improve Bly's writing. What they did not need to teach her was how to put a subject at ease or report compassionately on those whose lives seemed desperate and bleak.

Bly had these skills, earned in part during the hard years after she left school.

"If no amusement is offered them, they will seek it and accept the first presented," Bly wrote. "For the poor working girl, without friends, without money, with the ceaseless monotony of hard work, who shall condemn?"[9]

After the series concluded, so too did Bly's foray into the world of investigative journalism. She joined the ranks of the other female reporters—on the women's page.

Mexico!

Today, the newspaper section might be called "Life" or "Living." In others, it is "Style." Some label it "Arts and Entertainment," or "Show," or even "Home and Garden." It is where celebrity gossip, advice columns, and stories about the latest fashions appear. It is hidden by sections reserved for "hard news"—the facts about national crises and local events. It follows the opinion and sometimes even the sports pages. It is where the comics are found.

When Nellie Bly began her newspaper career, it went by one name. It was called "The Woman's Page." For the women contributing to the section, it was a dead end as surely as the menial jobs Bly endured.

Many books about Bly, especially those for younger readers, offer an explanation for her transfer similar to this one from 1998's *Encyclopedia of World Biography*: "While Bly's stories raised the indignation of Pittsburgh's citizens and inspired changes, the institutions she attacked were displeased and threatened to remove their advertisements from the newspaper. To appease their customers, the editors of the *Dispatch* changed the focus of Bly's writing, giving her cultural and social events to cover."[1]

Biographer Brooke Kroeger disagrees. "It is amusing to note that in personality sketches and juvenile biographies of Bly published long after her death," Kroeger writes,

> [The eight-part *Pittsburg Dispatch*] series is remembered as her indignant crusade to unmask the desperate conditions under which Pittsburgh's poor women were forced to labor. . . . Judged by the current standard, the articles read like a Chamber of Commerce booster pamphlet free from any criticism of the eight factories she toured. The only negative comments came from the women she interviewed in speaking about what happened to them on their last jobs—at factories Bly neither named nor visited in her subsequent reports.[2]

Far from angering the powers of Pittsburgh, however, Bly may have simply run out of ideas. Her first two pieces derived from personal experience. Her eight-part series on female factory workers may have, temporarily, exhausted her idea file. Shifting to the women's page meant covering scheduled stories—like flower shows—and interviewing notable people.

She could not do what beginning male reporters often did—cover crime and politics. In the 1880s, those arenas were seen as inappropriate for a woman. In a later interview with Bly, the *New York Herald*'s publisher, Dr. George H. Hepworth, said he would not allow a female reporter to cover the police or criminal courts because anyone she interviewed would give her "as little information as they could to get rid of her." Besides, he added, "a gentleman could not in delicacy ask a woman to have anything to do with that class of news."[3]

She authored a piece celebrating Governor Robert E. Pattison's proclaiming April 16 as Arbor Day, which encouraged Pennsylvanians to plant more trees, and noted it was the first time the state had acted to preserve trees in two centuries. Bly's byline appeared on articles about the annual flower show and women's clothing. She also did general interest reporting profiling the Economites—the thrifty residents of Economy, Pennsylvania.

Bly interviewed the first woman to own an opera company and profiled a chorus girl. Although chorus girls were considered "low" women of poor moral character, Bly's gift for compassionate interviewing encouraged her subject to open up about her life. She discussed chorus girls who make new "mashes" in every new town on their tour and the men who waited by the theater's exit door offering them presents and love letters. Some men gave the women money; some women formed intimate relationships with the men. Yet most chorus girls dated within their theater company.

Bly's eye for telling detail was immediately apparent. Readers might imagine a chorus girl as "a big, loud-voiced, flashily dressed, ill-bred woman who would rather be dressed in pink tights than petticoats—a woman devoid of all principle, who lived for the show," the reporter wrote. Instead, her subject was "a pretty, dark-eyed, golden-haired lass of probably twenty-one summers; a slender, girlish form clad in a light blue dress with a plain white-lined collar around her throat, the golden hair brushed back, dressed in two braids, displaying an intelligent forehead."[4]

After a year of feature writing, Bly was bored. She wanted adventure, not the women's page. She decided to quit. In early 1886, she left Pittsburgh to write stories hundreds of miles away.

PLANS

Although she quit as a full-time reporter, Bly's byline continued in the *Dispatch*. She needed all the money she could earn. Working as a freelance writer, she could write for whomever she wanted. Instead of a salary, she was paid by the article. Bly had sacrificed security for freedom. This choice would become familiar.

Before quitting the *Dispatch*, Bly had listened at her mother's house as Baltimore and Ohio Railroad workers like Tom Smiley and Tony Orr described their travels. The two sometimes took Bly out on the town. Whether or not one, or both of them, formed a romantic relationship with her is unknown. Bly's private life was very secretive. When a florist asked if she knew the language of flowers, Bly replied that it was a language she had never learned. "Well, you never have been very much in love with a particular man," he replied.[5]

Besides taking her around Pittsburgh, Smiley and Orr pulled boyish pranks on young Nellie. After stringing chairs together in the darkened hallway, they waited until Bly entered, laughing as she stumbled over them.

(opposite page) Relegated to the women's page, Nellie Bly wrote articles on topics like Arbor Day and fashion. For one article, she interviewed a chorus girl, like the one pictured here. Such performers had a poor reputation in the nineteenth century, but Bly was able to get the woman to open up by putting her at ease.

She was not amused. Still, their stories inspired wander-lust. She imagined boarding a train, taking it as far as the tracks allowed. The question was: Where?

A visiting Mexican delegation provided the answer. Assigned to show them around Pittsburgh, Bly earned an invitation to visit their country.

Since it was considered improper and dangerous for a single woman to travel alone, Bly persuaded her mother to accompany her. The two left in February 1886. Not only

PRESIDENT PORFIRIO DÍAZ

"After half a century of independence [Mexico's] economy lay ruined, its people were exhausted by civil war and over half its territory had been lost to the United States," the *Encyclopedia of World Biography* notes. "Into this chaos, José Porfirio Díaz radically changed the government and the economy."*

The son of a veterinarian, Díaz became a guerrilla fighter, a sugar farmer, and the owner of a furniture factory. Today he is best remembered for presiding over a period of such dynamic economic growth that it is called the *Porfiriato*, in his honor.

Elected president in 1876, Díaz promised to govern for a single term. Instead, his handpicked successor, General Manuel González, sold land and mineral rights to foreign businesses while helping his friends get rich. The country teetered toward bankruptcy. González himself made millions.

Díaz returned to the presidency, where he remained until his overthrow in 1911. "Out of bankruptcy, he established credit; he put up schools," Dolores Butterfield wrote the year Díaz left office. "He invited foreign capital into his country and made did Bly not speak the language of flowers, she did not speak the language of Mexico.

MEXICAN MEDDLING

It took Bly four days to reach Mexico's border. In her first pieces for the *Pittsburg Dispatch*, she joined the long line of writers complimenting President Porfirio Díaz. "New buildings are rapidly going up," she wrote, "old ones being repaired and Eastern people opening up stores. Everything

it possible for foreign capital to go in. . . . There were railroads and telegraphs; the cities were graced with beautiful edifices, with theatres and parks, with electricity and asphalt. . . . But all this was only a shell. . . . The economic condition of the Mexican lower classes was not touched—the process of 'nation building' seemed not to include them. In the shadow of a modern civilization stalked poverty and ignorance worthy of the middle ages." Díaz would oversee the production of 800 million barrels of oil annually and the laying of 16,000 miles (25,750 kilometers) of train track, but the standard of living for the poor actually decreased.**

---

* "José de la Cruz Porfirio Díaz." *Encyclopedia of World Biography*, 2nd ed. 17 Vols. Gale Research, 1998. Reproduced in *Biography Resource Center*. Farmington Hills, Mich.: Gale, 2010.

** E.A. Tweedie and Dolores Butterfield. "The Downfall of Díaz; Mexico Plunges into Revolution." 1911. *The Great Events by Famous Historians*, Vol. 21. Harrogate, Tenn.: The National Alunmi, 1926. *World Book Online Reference Center.*

has a brisk look as if money were plenty. President Díaz has been having plans made by which the city may be drained better. The streets are swept daily and no garbage is permitted to collect on them."[6]

The articles she wrote were similar to ones appearing in twenty-first-century Sunday Travel sections. She wrote about bullfighting and how "there is but one thing that poor and rich indulge in with equal delight and pleasure—that is cigarette smoking. Those tottering with age down to the creeping babe are continually smoking. No spot in Mexico is sacred from them; in churches, on the railway cars, on the streets, in the theaters—everywhere are to be seen men and women—of the *elite*—smoking."[7]

She described tortilla makers who "spit on their hands to keep the dough from sticking, and bake in a pan of hot grease, kept boiling by a few lumps of charcoal. Rich and poor buy and eat them, apparently unmindful of the way they are made. . . . Many [Americans] surprise the Mexicans by refusing even a taste after they see the bakers."[8]

She may have had a relationship with U.S. writer Joaquin Miller. After Bly discovered a street where every doorway led to a coffin maker, he complimented her, "Little Nell, you are a second Columbus. You have discovered a street that has no like in the world and I have been over the world twice."[9]

Even as she wrote light articles, storm clouds gathered. After a poor engineer named Jacob Heiney died, the Mexican Government Office of Deputation refused to release his body. Heiney had grown up in Allegheny County, Pennsylvania, and was the sole support of his elderly father. He was also a U.S. citizen.

After an American "indignation committee" was organized, U.S. Legation Minister Henry R. Jackson stepped in to secure the body's release. It still took five hours. Bly reported that "after the burial [of Heiney], a sensation was created by a leak that the body had been taken from

Except for one four-year period, Porfirio Díaz ruled Mexico
from 1876 to 1911. During her trip to Mexico in 1886, Nellie Bly
initially wrote articles complimentary of Díaz and what he had
done for Mexico. Later articles, however, criticized the government, and she was forced to leave the country earlier than she
had planned.

its coffin and when officials went to replace it they found it had swollen until it was too large to go in. So the arms and legs were cut off and the breast split open so it could be doubled up." If that article did not win Bly fans in the Mexican government, the one she wrote on March 22 led them to threaten her with prison.[10]

Bly did not speak Spanish. Some of the best English speakers—not to mention the top sources for information—were local reporters and editors. It was natural she would interact with them and develop stories based upon their suggestions.

Bly soon learned that editors and reporters who questioned Mexico's government faced imprisonment. She wrote an article describing with horror the arrest of a Mexico City newspaper editor. His only crime, she protested, was criticizing the government—something he should be able to do in a democratic society.

After appearing in the *Pittsburg Dispatch*, her article was reprinted in the *St. Louis Globe-Democrat*. When a copy made its way to Mexican officials, Bly's time there was numbered. "I had some regard for my health," she admitted later, "and a Mexican jail is the least desirable abode on the face of the earth, so some care was exercised in the selection of topics while we were inside their gates."[11]

Bly wrote:

> An American, at the hands of the Mexican authorities, suffers all the tortures that some preachers delight to tell us some human beings will find in the world to come. . . . Two meals, not enough to sustain life in a sick cat, must suffice him for an entire week. There are no beds, and not even water. Prisoners also have the not very comfortable knowledge that, if they get too troublesome, the keepers have a nasty habit of making them stand up and be shot in the back. The reports made out in these cases are "shot while trying to escape."[12]

Her time spent in the foreign country led to Bly's book *Six Months in Mexico*. Before it was released in 1888, she revealed the stories she could not reveal while a foreigner in a foreign land.

A LITTLE CULTURE

Her trip began as an adventure. As weeks stretched into months, it grew tedious. She longed for her life in the United States. Despite her meager finances, life in Pittsburgh was comfortable by comparison. She missed her own bed and was sick of eating chili-stuffed meat, fried pumpkins stuffed with chilies, and other stomach-upsetting foods. She planned to spend six months in the country, but her plans were altered by her issues with the government.

On June 22, Bly left the Panhandle Express for a train station platform in Pittsburgh. Met by a reporter from the *Dispatch*, Bly did not even wait to submit her own copy. Instead, she unleashed a stinging commentary directed toward the country she had just left. Although she had met kind and helpful Mexicans, Bly felt that most of them were cruel and uncivilized, possessing "a sort of horror for everything that comes from the United States."[13]

She focused her wrath on cowardly newspapers in Mexico that were unwilling to stand up to the government. Throughout the summer, Bly's articles were radically different from the fluffy pieces she wrote in Mexico.

Describing Díaz's government as corrupt and dangerous, Bly included allegations from "men whom I know to be honorable" along with her own experiences.

That such things missed the public press will rather astonish Americans who are used to a free press; but the Mexican papers never publish one word against the government or officials and the people who are at their mercy dare not breath one word against them, as those in position are more able than the most tyrannical czar to make their lives miserable.[14]

Near the conclusion of her book *Six Months in Mexico*, Bly wrote, "The Mexicans have a good deal of suppressed wrath bothering them at the present day; they know that Díaz is a tyrannical czar, and want to overthrow him." Bly's prediction of Díaz's overthrow came true more than two decades later.[15]

"It was natural and inevitable that a Government in which there was never any change or movement should stagnate and become corrupt," Dolores Butterfield wrote in 1911. "Porfirio Díaz was not a President, but, in all save the name, an absolute monarch, and inevitably there formed about his throne a cordon of men as unpatriotic and self-interested as he may have been patriotic and disinterested—as to a great extent he undeniably was."[16]

Bly possessed a newcomer's zeal for the power of the press. Mexico's state-subsidized newspapers were so disliked that Bly claimed men would not even use one "to hide behind in a street car when some woman with a dozen bundles, three children and two baskets is looking for a seat."[17]

Bly was appalled by Mexican newspapers, but for her the *Pittsburg Dispatch* was not much of an improvement. After a summer contributing articles about Mexico, she was rewarded with a new position. Nellie Bly became a theater and arts reporter.

BLY'S NEW SUIT

As far as Nellie Bly was concerned, Colonel Samuel Jackson was a thief. Instead of a robber's gun, he wielded pen and paper. For more than a decade he administered the $5,000 that Judge Michael Cochran left for the care of his minor children. He also paid Mary Jane Cochrane the widow's interest on $2,650—what he paid when he bought the late judge's home.

Bly's issues with Jackson reached the Armstrong County courthouse in the fall of 1886 when she filed suit against him. Testimony from Bly and other family members—along with the colonel himself—revealed the depth of his financial mismanagement.

He claimed to have recorded all deposits and withdrawals on paper. This was difficult to verify—he kept the estate's money in his personal accounts. He could not prove he had not used the Cochrane money for his own expenses.

Jackson's poor record keeping was emphasized during his testimony when he claimed Bly had attended the Indiana Normal School for two semesters. She did not complete the first one.

Bly testified along with her mother, Mary Jane Cochrane, her brother Charles and her sister Kate that their signatures were forged. Besides receipts they claimed never to have seen, the colonel had illegally given money to Bly's stepfather, Jack Ford, from the estate.

The court appointed an auditor. The audit and legal motions took more than two years. By then Bly had decided the meager return was not worth her time. Jackson's reputation was damaged enough that others would not trust their money with him.

Even as the Armstrong County Court appointed an auditor, Bly returned to the *Dispatch* in October 1886. Her coverage of theater people was not radically different from twenty-first-century profiles of film and television stars. Bly authored a column, "Footlight Gossip," which looked backstage at various Pittsburgh productions and another one, "Among the Artists," examining the work of local artists. Bly used the second as a forum to criticize Pittsburgh's rich for not using their money to promote the arts as the wealthy of other cities did.

Bly was not doing the kind of reporting that interested her. A promotion to lead culture reporter in early 1887 did little to change this.

Erasmus Wilson prompted the adversarial letter that began Bly's writing career. Despite authoring "The Quiet Observer" column criticizing women in the workplace, Wilson became Bly's champion. She went to him with her concerns. Later, he remembered, "The city editor couldn't find anything to her taste and they jarred and fussed a good deal."[18]

In March 1887, the bustling offices of the *Dispatch* were interrupted by a search for Bly. She was usually punctual and rarely absent. Wilson remembered that "no one knew where she was, until the following note was discovered: Dear Q.O. —I am off for New York. Look out for me. Bly."[19]

Despite having been a staff reporter for less than a year, Bly headed to the largest city in the United States without a job offer or decent contacts. It was a place where reporters with much more experience often failed.

Nellie Bly Takes On the World

After leaving her job at the *Pittsburg Dispatch*, Nellie Bly's confidence faded. In May 1887, she settled into a tiny furnished room at 15 West 96th Street in Manhattan—one of New York City's five boroughs. Located in a rough neighborhood, the apartment had a solitary window offering a grim view of the building's back alley. As the promise of spring faded into the hot reality of summer, that bleak vista was a constant reminder to Bly that she had not succeeded.

In the late 1880s, New York was developing into a modern metropolis. Benefiting from its natural harbor, it flourished as imports and exports, traders and travelers, came and went on ships unable to traverse the shallower waterways farther inland. Along the southern tip of Manhattan, nearly one-quarter of all the banking resources in the country could be found. Across the city, nearly 8,000 manufacturers employed more than 130,000 workers.

In the United States some 3 million immigrants arrived from 1865 to 1873. Already boasting well over 1 million residents, the largest city in the United States was home to many thousands of them. In 1886, the French-donated Statue of Liberty was erected in New York Harbor as a beacon to new arrivals. They traveled from countries like Ireland, Germany, and Italy imagining the "American Dream" of financial success and personal freedom. Most settled into cramped tenements and difficult, low-paying jobs.

"Construction breakthroughs involving the use of iron shell framing and improved load-bearing supports made it structurally feasible to build higher, while such innovations as the passenger lift or elevator made tall buildings practical," author Thomas Kessner explains. "The result ushered in not only a new skyline, but a change in urban scale." As one observer joked, "When they find themselves a little crowded, they simply tilt a street on end and call it a skyscraper."[1]

Clustered around City Hall, the impressive buildings of Park Row housed the *New York Tribune, Times, Herald, Journal, Sun,* and *Mail and Express* along with a number of others. By 1890, the tallest building along "Newspaper Row" would be the home of the *New York World.*

The building was 309 feet (94 meters) high. When it was completed, the New York World Building was the highest office building on Earth. Not long after its completion, it became better known by a different name. It was called the Pulitzer Building.

PULITZER'S PRESS

Like most large cities in the late 1800s, New York boasted numerous daily newspapers. There were lesser papers, like

In the late 1800s, the buildings on Park Row near City Hall in Manhattan housed many of New York's newspapers. The building on the far left was the New York World Building, also known as the Pulitzer Building. Many an aspiring reporter, including Nellie Bly, hoped to be able to walk through its doors.

the *New York Tribune* and the *Mail and Express*, along with the now best known—the *New York Times*—which a century ago had none of its current power and prestige. The most successful papers, the *New York Sun* and the *New York Herald*, catered to an elite, educated readership.

A Hungarian immigrant, Joseph Pulitzer left home at 17 and was soon rejected by several European armies.

Recruited by the Union army in 1864, Pulitzer jumped ship as soon as he reached Boston. Enlisting on his own earned the young man a larger signing bonus.

That template for making money endured. Working as a clerk for several law firms, he learned enough to become a lawyer himself. Successful at that profession, he put his savings into the buying and selling of newspapers.

In the 1880s, Pulitzer rapidly transformed the *New York World* into a successful newspaper. Four years after he purchased it, the *World*'s Sunday circulation increased from 20,000 to 200,000.

Just over 100 years later, Australian Rupert Murdoch developed a cable news channel catering to a group he felt was underrepresented by competitors. Murdoch's *Fox News* focused on conservatives, presenting news in a colorful, unconventional format. Pulitzer focused on immigrants and the working poor.

The *New York World* was written in English—a second language for many of its readers. In the words of one commentator, "He taught them how to be Americans."[2]

Pulitzer pioneered the use of headlines and was the first to use bold, large print to separate them from the rest of the type. He made front pages more compelling while offering reader contests and gruesome accounts of heinous crimes. He introduced "yellow journalism," with its sensational reporting style. The *World*'s competitors generally supported Republicans; his championed Democrats. And because he paid higher wages than his rivals, the *World* attracted some of the era's best reporters and editors.

The *World*'s growing circulation and reputation made it Nellie Bly's top choice for a reporting job. She could not even get an interview.

Just as they do today, in 1887 writers from across the country dreamed of working for a top New York publication. It was the big leagues in a city that was the center of

Joseph Pulitzer bought the *New York World* in the 1880s and turned it into a successful newspaper. As the newspaper's primary audience, Pulitzer targeted New York City's new immigrant community and the working poor.

the country's publishing industry—not just newspapers, but magazines and books as well. The top newspapers had more readers and won more awards than those anywhere else in the United States. Every day reporters from smaller cities and towns across the country arrived in New York with clips and letters of recommendation. Every day the former star reporters from places like Atlanta, Des Moines, and Cleveland left unable to land a position.

Bly had less than two years of reporting experience. Even more challenging, she was a woman who did not want to cover flower shows. She could not get past the *World*'s front door.

Today job seekers must get past "gatekeepers"—the receptionists, editorial assistants, even interns who work for editors and publishers. Among their many duties, they prevent applicants from interrupting their bosses. When Bly was trying to get a job, the process was even less civilized. Like nightclub bouncers, large men restricted access to the buildings lining Newspaper Row.

Bly's situation was turning desperate. "I was penniless," she wrote. "I was too proud to return to the position I had left in search of new worlds to conquer. Indeed, I cannot say the thought ever presented itself to me, for I have never in my life turned back from a course I had started upon."[3]

Without abandoning the city, Bly returned to writing for the *Pittsburg Dispatch*. Finances left her little choice. Her former employer already had a male correspondent in New York, however, so Bly was forced to write feature articles about topics she loathed. Harder news remained the beat of reporter George N. McCain.

After a month of writing "puff pieces," August arrived with a fresh opportunity. Whether or not she created it is unclear.

Bly claimed to have received a letter from a woman interested in newspaper reporting. She wondered if New York City was the best place to embark upon her career. Instead of answering, Bly wrote an article interviewing men she called "the newspaper gods of Gotham." Her background as a reporter from Pittsburgh enabled her to speak with a number of top editors. She also posed as a job applicant.[4]

During Bly's first foray "undercover," the *New York Herald*'s Dr. George H. Hepworth conceded that his paper would not use a woman for crime reporting. He believed most men would be uncomfortable speaking to her. Besides, he was too much of a gentleman to assign such an unpleasant job to a woman.

Besides Hepworth, Bly quoted editors from the *Telegram*, the *Mail and Express* and the *New York Sun*. At the *Sun*, Charles A. Dana said women were "not regarded with editorial favor" because most editors did not believe they were capable of accurate reporting—a journalist's most important qualification.[5]

Bly was finally able to get past the front door of the *New York World*. Colonel John A. Cockerill agreed with his editorial brethren. Women were best suited for "society coverage," he claimed, mentioning the reporting Bly loathed. Perhaps noticing Bly's distaste, he admitted that most women did not want to do it. "A man is of far greater service," Cockerill offered, adding that the *World* had two female staff writers: "So you see we do not object personally."[6]

Although discouraging, the story provided an opportunity. First published in the *Pittsburg Dispatch*, Bly's article was reprinted in Boston and quoted in the *Journalist*. The trade paper was read by many in the newspaper business. Her article responding to an aspiring female journalist—whether or not that journalist was actually Bly herself—demonstrated her motto: "Energy rightly applied and directed will accomplish anything."[7]

Unfortunately Bly's energy was running out as quickly as her money. There were no job offers, not even from the papers where she had posed as an applicant.

A SHOT AT THE *WORLD*

On August 27, 1887, Nellie Bly's article was quoted in New York's own *Mail and Express*. The piece described her as a "bright and talented young woman who has done a great deal of good writing for the newspapers."[8]

The impact of that uplifting description was tempered by Bly losing her purse—along with her last bit of money from the *Dispatch* articles. She refocused her energy on writing for the *New York World*. Walking to its offices in the late-summer heat was unbearable; she persuaded her landlady to lend her money for a ride. If the *World* did not hire her, she would have to leave New York.

Bly once again had four stories to ascend on a Sunday hoping to become a reporter. Two-and-a-half years later, her ambition was no different; neither was her desperation. At least the *New York World* had an elevator.

This time, the gatekeepers allowed her entry. Bly's name had appeared in a rival paper; she told anyone who interfered that she had a story. If the *World* did not want it, another newspaper would.

After Bly sat down across from Colonel Cockerill, he realized she did not really have a story. What she had were a few fantastic, wildly impractical ideas.

She wanted the *World* to send her to Europe. From there she could travel back to the United States just as many immigrants did—in steerage. The cheapest and least comfortable accommodations on a boat, steerage was how the poor made the transatlantic crossing. Bly would write about the experience.

Cockerill listened as she pitched other ideas, each one "as desperate as they were startling to carry out." Although he doubted any of them were feasible, he did not want to lose Bly to a rival. That day he did not give her an assignment. He gave her money.[9]

With $25 in her pocket as a retainer, she was to return on September 22. By then he would know if the paper could use her; in the meantime she was not to take a job with a competitor.

On the appointed date, Bly met with Cockerill. She did not know what to expect, but his cash advance seemed like a good sign. He told her the ideas she had pitched were too elaborate for a first assignment. Besides, he wanted her to write a local story.

The growth in the *World*'s circulation was partly due to the paper's risk-taking. Its stories were often edgy, its reporters expected to take chances.

Bly knew she might have to take on dangerous assignments to join the *World* staff. Cockerill had one. He wanted her to go to Blackwell's Island.

THE ISLAND

Located in New York City's East River, Blackwell's Island stretched across 120 acres. Alongside separate facilities for prisoners and a charity hospital was the notorious "insane asylum," where the mentally ill were kept against their will. Over the summer, a number of New York papers had written about conditions at the facility. Articles in the *New York Times* included charges leveled by a number of young nurses who felt that doctors had behaved inappropriately toward them. The *World*'s editorials demanded an investigation into the treatment of patients.

Cockerill did not want Bly to interview a few doctors, staff members, or even patients. He was not asking her to approach Blackwell's Island as a reporter. He wanted her to be a patient. He wanted her to get herself committed.

"Stunt reporting" or "detective reporting" played an important part in "New Journalism" and the *World*'s success. The reporter did not just cover the story. The reporter *became* the story.

With that method criticized for its sensational elements, reporters today are discouraged from posing as someone else. Most newspapers prohibit it. Television newsmagazines like *60 Minutes* and *Dateline*, however, still use it. For Bly it was a unique opportunity. Only a woman could be a patient in the hospital's female wing, and only a reporter with her background could be expected to succeed. Bly would rather be committed to an asylum than cover another flower show.

Cockerill emphasized one point: "We do not ask you to go there for the purpose of making sensational revelations." Instead, he wanted her to "write up things as you find them, good or bad; give praise or blame as you think best. . . . But, I am afraid of that chronic smile of yours."

IN HER OWN WORDS

Nellie Bly had the confidence that she could complete her first assignment for the *New York World*:

> Did I think I had the courage to go through such an ordeal as the mission would demand? Could I assume the characteristics of insanity to such a degree that I could pass the doctors, live for a week among the insane without the authorities there finding out that I was only a [reporter]. I said I believed I could. . . .
>
> My instructions were simply to go on with my work as soon as I felt that I was ready. I was to chronicle faithfully the experiences I underwent, and . . . describe [the asylum's] inside workings, which are always so effectually hidden by white-capped nurses, as well as by bolts and bars, from the knowledge of the public.*

* Nellie Bly, *Ten Days in a Mad-House*. New York: American Publishers/N.L. Munro, 1888, p. 7.

"I will smile no more," Bly promised.[10]

She planned to begin her ruse the very next day. She spent a sleepless night preparing. Knowing doctors would examine her, "I feared that they could not be deceived," she wrote. "I began to think my task a hopeless one; but it had to be done."[11]

She opened her eyes wide, staring unblinking at her reflection. "I assure you the sight was not reassuring, even to myself, especially in the dead of night." She began to sweat, despite the evening's chill. "Between times, practicing before the mirror and picturing my future as a lunatic, I read snatches of improbable and impossible ghost stories, so that when the dawn came to chase away the night, I felt that I was in a fit mood for my mission."[12]

Her charade began on Second Avenue. For thirty cents a night she was given room and board at Matron Irene Stenard's Temporary Home for Women. Bly told a judge "the eating was the worst I ever tried." The food she ate at the Stenard Home would be gourmet fare compared with the meals to come.[13]

Like the working poor Bly profiled in Pittsburgh, the women she shared lodging with were predominantly factory workers. They endured a woman who did not know where she came from, had no job, and feared the house was filled with killers. Bly's behavior was so convincing that the first woman assigned to share her room "declared that she would not stay with that 'crazy woman' for all the money of the Vanderbilts."[14]

Bly's eventual roommate was a former proofreader named Ruth Caine. The older woman did all she could to help the undercover reporter sleep. Instead, the writer suffered another sleepless night, worried that in her sleep she might give away her true identity. Exhaustion would add realism to her portrayal.

Unable to read or write while undercover, Bly contemplated "the story of my life. Old friends were recalled with a pleasurable thrill; old enmities, old heartaches, old joys were once again present. The turned-down pages of my life were turned up and the past was present." She thought about the ways her life would change if her quest succeeded. It was, she later wrote, "the greatest night of my existence. For a few hours I stood face to face with 'self.' "[15]

The gray dawn brought Bly diverting entertainment in the form of hungry cockroaches. Caine awoke and tried to help the young woman she knew as Nellie Brown, the name Cockerill chose for its similarity to her byline. Even better, the initials matched the ones her laundry placed inside her clothing.

Bly told Caine—and anyone else who listened—that she would not leave without her trunks. The women knew Bly had arrived empty-handed.

Irene Stenard called the police. Accompanied by Stenard, Bly was taken away by two officers. She wrote that the four "walked along very quietly and finally came to the station house, which the good woman [Mrs. Stenard] assured me was the express office, and that there we should certainly find my missing effects. I went inside with fear and trembling, for good reason."[16]

Once there, Bly feared exposure. The police captain had met her as a reporter. Her ruse undetected, Bly was sent to the Essex Market Police Courtroom, where a police officer explained, "Here's the express office. We shall soon find those trunks of yours."[17]

Judge Duffy was sympathetic. Bly was wearing an outfit she considered threadbare and shoddy, the kind of rags a crazy person would wear. She was actually better dressed than most of the women there. A *Sun* reporter later described her as a "modest, comely girl of nineteen with [a] low, mild voice and cultivated manner handsomely dressed in a brown-trimmed frock of gray flannel with the sleeves cut in the latest style, accessorized by brown silk gloves and a black straw sailor's hat trimmed in brown and veiled in thin gray illusion."[18]

She failed to look impoverished but succeeded in behaving irrationally. When the judge asked if her accent was Cuban, Bly agreed, claiming her name was Nellie Moreno (which is Spanish for "brown").

After a police officer said Bly should be sent "to the Island," Mrs. Stenard argued, "She is a lady, and it would kill her to be put on the Island."[19]

Bly was upset at the boardinghouse matron's interference. "There has been some foul work here," the judge offered. "I believe this child has been drugged and brought to this city. Make out the papers and we will send her to Bellevue for examination."[20]

Before that happened, the *Sun* reporter tried to interview Bly. She had met him before and managed to have him sent away before he recognized her. On September 25 the *New York Sun*'s front-page headline asked, "Who Is This Insane Girl?"[21]

ON THE ISLAND

At Bellevue, a doctor examining Bly considered her enlarged pupils a sign of insanity. She was just nearsighted. Dr. William C. Braisted told the *New York Herald*, "[Bly's] delusions, her dull apathetic condition, the muscular twitching of her arms and her loss of memory, all indicate hysteria," but its rival, the *New York Sun*, quoted Bellevue's warden, William B. O'Rourke, who felt the young woman was faking insanity. O'Rourke's is the only known dissenting opinion.[22]

After a few more restless nights, Bly was taken to a dirty and foul-smelling ferry. As the boat headed toward the asylum, she may have contemplated her last conversation with

Cockerill. "How will you get me out," she had asked, "after I once get in?"

"I do not know," he replied, "but we will get you out if we have to tell who you are, and for what purpose you feigned insanity—only get in."[23]

Disembarking, she was led to an ambulance.

"'What is this place?' I asked of the man, who had his fingers sunk into the flesh of my arm.

'Blackwell's Island, an insane place, where you'll never get out of.'" Thus was Bly greeted on her first day as a patient on "The Island."[24]

For 10 days Bly posed as a "lunatic." She realized that, once a doctor determined a woman was insane, few would question his diagnosis.

The reporter witnessed immigrants condemned to the asylum because they could not understand the English-speaking doctors. Bly wrote about the time she "read a motto on the wall, 'While I live I hope.' The absurdity of it struck me forcibly. I would have liked to put above the gates that open to the asylum, 'He who enters here leaveth hope behind.'"[25]

Before reporting on the inhumane conditions within Blackwell's, Nellie Bly endured them. It was worse than she imagined. She sacrificed privacy, safety, and any hope of comfort.

"We were taken into a cold, wet bathroom, and I was ordered to undress," she recalled. "Did I protest? Well, I never grew so earnest in my life as when I tried to beg off. They said if I did not they would use force and that it would not be very gentle."[26]

"At last everything was gone excepting one garment. 'I will not remove it,' I said vehemently, but they took it off. I gave one glance to the group of patients gathered at the door watching the scene, and I jumped into the bathtub with more energy than grace."[27]

This illustration from the 1860s shows patients in the yard of the asylum at Blackwell's Island. In 1887, Nellie Bly was able to get inside the asylum undercover by pretending to be insane. The conditions that she endured there were much less idyllic than this picture suggests.

The water was ice cold and used by a number of women before it was replaced. Bly was scrubbed by another patient, then handed a towel as well used as the water.

Before she was even dried, she was put into a slip. Asking an attendant for a nightgown, Bly was told, "You are in a public institution now, and you can't expect to get anything. This is a charity, and you should be thankful for what you get."

Bly knew that this was the attitude of many, both inside and out. "But the city pays to keep these places up," she argued, "and pays people to be kind to the unfortunates brought here."

The woman promised Bly "you don't need to expect any kindness here, for you won't get it." Her words were prophecy.[28]

Bly witnessed patients beaten by nurses who used other patients as lookouts. She saw the nurses enjoy fresh fruit a few feet from women fed with rancid butter, moldy bread, and spoiled meat. And she witnessed doctors diagnosing everyone they saw as "insane." In her book *Ten Days in a Mad-House*, Bly later wrote, "The insane asylum on Blackwell's Island is a human rat trap. It is easy to get in, but once there it is impossible to get out. I had intended to have myself committed to the violent wards, the Lodge and Retreat, but . . . I decided not to risk my health."[29]

RELEASED

Nellie Brown had a visitor. She went to him nervously, knowing it was too soon for the *New York World* to spring her from the asylum.

It was a reporter. He had pretended to be looking for a loved one. He was really following up on the story about a young girl named Nellie who had been recently committed.

"I went to the sitting room at the end of the hall, and there sat a gentleman who had known me intimately for years," Bly wrote. She whispered to the man, "Don't give me away." Bly told the woman who had brought her down that she did not know the man.

The reporter went along with Bly's ruse. "This is not the young lady I came in search of."[30]

On October 4, the visitor she *was* waiting for arrived. Peter A. Hendricks was an attorney hired by the *World*. The staff of the asylum allowed him to take Bly into his care.

Soon the *World's* competitors learned that "Nellie Brown" had been released. They did not suspect she was a reporter. A *Times* article claimed she had been cured.

On October 9, the *New York World* published Bly's account of her experiences. The only people more embarrassed than the hoodwinked reporters were the doctors who had declared Bly insane. Running on the first page of the Sunday Features section, her story covered two full pages. Bly's byline appeared at the article's conclusion. In the late nineteenth century many new reporters, male or female, reported anonymously.

The *Sun* ran a front-page article with the headline, "Playing the Mad Woman: Nellie Bly Too Sharp for the Island Doctors." Blackwell's doctors and other staff members were quoted, questioning the accuracy of her reporting. Despite their objections, the prominent placement of Bly's name increased her notoriety while the article's description of her as "intelligent, capable, and self-reliant," increased her prestige.[31]

When the second part of the *World's* series ran, Nellie Bly was no longer a byline at the conclusion of an article. She was part of the headline: "Inside the Madhouse: Nellie Bly's Experience in Blackwell's Island Asylum."[32]

The *World* also challenged the physicians quoted in the *Sun's* article. The headline said it all: "All the Doctors Fooled."[33]

Undercover

Among other abuses taken up for investigation by the pres-
ent Grand Jury are those alleged to exist in the female insane
asylum at Blackwell's Island. The Grand Jury, accompanied
by Assistant District Attorney [Vernon] Davis and Nellie Bly,
the young woman who recently spent a week in the asylum
for the purpose of investigation, visited the asylum yesterday
and spent most of the day there. The result of the trip will be
made known in a presentment at the end of the month.[1]

—"Taken Up by the Grand Jury,"
New York Times, October 20, 1887

"Soon after I had bidden farewell to the Blackwell's Island Insane Asylum, I was summoned to appear before the grand jury," Nellie Bly later wrote in her book

Ten Days in a Mad-House. "I answered the summons with pleasure, because I longed to help those of God's most unfortunate children whom I had left prisoners behind me. If I could not bring them that boon of all boons, liberty, I hoped to at least influence others to make life more bearable for them."[2]

The second time she took a boat to Blackwell's, it was as an advocate joined by the men who formed the grand jury along with the district attorney. Rather than traveling upon a dirty ferry bound for the asylum, Bly rode upon a clean, new vessel—the one she had taken before was supposedly being repaired.

Their journey was supposed to be a secret. It was not.

The group discovered fresh bread laid out before the patients. The non-English speakers were no longer interred. To Bly the facility seemed cleaner.

A doctor claimed an abusive nurse had been fired. Besides, he had no way of knowing how cold the bath water was or how many women used it before it was changed. Bly learned the doctor had an hour's warning before the group's arrival—not enough for radical changes, but enough time to prepare.

Bly was worried. Would her article even be believed? Then a patient came forward.

Anne Neville "knew me only as Miss Nellie Brown," Bly recalled, "and was wholly ignorant of my story." Neville had accompanied the reporter on her first boat trip to the island.[3]

Neville told the jurors:

When Miss Brown and I were brought here the nurses were cruel and the food was too bad to eat. We did not have enough clothing and Miss Brown asked for more all the time. I thought she was very kind, for when a doctor promised her some clothing she said she would give it to me. Strange to say, ever since Miss Brown has been taken away everything is different. The nurses are very kind and we are given plenty to wear. The doctors come to see us often and the food is greatly improved.[4]

Most likely doctors and the staff members on Blackwell's Island had read Bly's articles and began to make improvements. She feared the changes would be temporary. Her fears were unfounded. Not only did the grand jury agree with Bly's assessment of the asylum, along with the changes her articles recommended, but it also felt that the budget for the Department of Public Charities and Corrections—which oversaw prisons, hospitals and other public charities—should be drastically increased. It was.

The department was given an increase of nearly $1 million; the money appropriated to Blackwell's Island was raised by nearly $60,000. Biographer Brooke Kroeger notes that "a consensus had been forming for some time to increase funding to the city's jails, hospitals, almshouses, workhouses, and asylums. Given the sensation her report caused, it is an allowable lapse into hyperbole to claim, as she did, that the additional funds came 'on the strength of my story.' She certainly had added valuable heft."[5]

Even as the grand jury's recommendations were implemented, Bly was working on other stories. She had been hired as a full-time staff reporter for the *New York World*.

HIRED

Joseph Pulitzer agreed with the decision by his editor, John Cockerill, to hire Bly, calling her "a very bright and very plucky new member of the staff." Impressed by her accomplishment, Pulitzer gave the young reporter "a handsome check" and predicted a great future for her.[6]

Others agreed. Across the country, newspapers picked up the story of the woman who feigned insanity and exposed the horrors of the asylum. In Canada, the *Hamilton Times* compared it to when "men and women were sent to insane asylums by doctors in collusion with relatives interested in having them put out of the way."[7]

A fellow reporter at the *Pittsburg Dispatch*, columnist Bessie Bramble, praised Bly for demonstrating "that cool courage, consummate craft and investigating ability are not monopolized by the brethren of the profession. By her clever woman's wit she has shown how easily men can be humbugged and imposed upon—and men hitherto deemed smart and experts at their business at that."[8]

Both "the mad house" and journalism offered additions to Bly's romantic life. During her incarceration at Blackwell's, she befriended Dr. Frank G. Ingram, who was the assistant superintendent of the facility. Presumably he was kinder than most of the others Bly met there, for she continued to see him after her release. During the same time, she also began to date *Life* magazine's drama critic, James Stetson Metcalfe. Bly's involvement with Metcalfe was serious enough that many expected the two to marry.

After inspiring Bly's letter to the *Pittsburg Dispatch*, columnist Erasmus Wilson had become her mentor during her tenure there. Following her Blackwell's Island exposé, she wrote to him about offers to give paid speeches. More unusual, her talent for pretending to be something other than a reporter inspired theater companies to want to hire Bly as an actress. She turned them down.

"So long as [being a reporter] pays," she wrote to Wilson. "They are very good to me in the *World* office and no one but Colonel Cockerill dare say a word to me. Somehow they treat me as if I was a pretty big girl." Bly signed the letter, "Your naughty kid, Nellie Bly."[9]

This 1881 painting by Fritz Paulsen is titled *At the Employment Agency of the Domestic Service Hiring Office*. Nellie Bly continued to work under-cover, posing for one assignment as a servant seeking work and exposing the disreputable practices of employment agencies for servants.

Despite not performing on a stage, the reporter con-tinued to act. Investigating employment agencies that were paid a fee to match housekeepers, maids, cooks, and other servants with employers, she wrote, "I had heard so many complaints from long-suffering mistresses, worked-out ser-vants, agencies and lawyers that I determined to investigate the subject to my own satisfaction."[10]

"There was only one way to do it," her article, "Trying to Be a Servant," continued.

That was to personate a servant and apply for a situation. I knew that there might be such things as "references" required, and, as I had never tested my abilities in this line, I did not know how to furnish them. Still, it would not do to allow a little thing like a "reference" to stop me in my work, and I would not ask any friend to commit herself to further my efforts."[11]

Bly arrived at the Germania Servants' Agency at 69 Fourth Avenue "dressed to look the character I wanted to represent." Hard beside a first floor whose accumulation of junk made Bly think of a secondhand store was a side door marked "Servants." Entering, she ascended a poorly maintained staircase, reaching the second floor and a door marked "Office." "I did not knock, but turned the knob of the door, and as it stuck top and bottom, I pressed my shoulder against it. It gave way, so did I, and I entered my career as a servant with a tumble."[12]

That embarrassing entrance revealed a small room decorated with cheap wallpaper and a dirty carpet. Even more disheartening was the sheet of paper affixed over the mantel declaring, "'References Investigated!!' with two exclamation points," Bly wrote. "Now if it had only been put quietly and mildly, or even with one exclamation point, but two—dreadful."[13]

Bly soon learned the quantity of exclamation points did not matter. Posing as Sally Lees, a recent arrival from Atlantic City, New Jersey, she told the employment agent that she did not have any local references.

He was not worried. He told her he could get her a job regardless, so long as she paid her $1 a month fee for the use of the agency and more money if he succeeded in finding her a decent position. Bly asked if he guaranteed he would find her work in the city. "Oh, certainly, certainly," he promised, "that's what this agency is for."[14]

Bly discovered that his word was as weak as the sign demanding references. Bly returned the next day to discover her services advertised in the *Tribune*. Soon after, "an aged gentleman" entered the agency. When he asked about

Bly's references, the agent replied, "She is an excellent girl and I can give you the best personal reference—the best of references."[15]

The gentleman was unwilling to pay Bly $14 a month. He only wanted to pay $10; the day before, the agent promised Bly he would get her work paying $20. The agent tried to sell the man use of the agency's listing for $2 a month. He quickly left.

Bly remained. All day she met other women her age: all of them unhappy, all of them unemployed. The agent offered out-of-town work to those who wanted to remain in New York while claiming no work was available for those willing to travel. As unpleasant as the first agency was, the second Bly visited was worse. Some 50 women were crammed into a series of small rooms, all of them waiting for jobs that never seemed to come.

For the *Pittsburg Dispatch*, Bly had interviewed factory managers and the women they employed. For the *New York World*, Bly planned something different: "I had often wondered at the tales of poor pay and cruel treatment that working girls tell," Bly wrote in "As a White Slave." "There was one way of getting at the truth. . . . It was becoming myself a paper box factory girl. Accordingly, I started out in search of work without experience, reference or aught to aid me."[16]

Her lack of experience or references was a greater detriment than at the agencies. The larger box factories believed Bly would just get in the way—even working for free. The women were trained by friends who undertook the task without extra pay. Finally, at a smaller factory, Bly got her chance.

She was led up five flights of stairs to a dimly lit, unventilated room reeking of glue fumes. Rows of women, some younger than 16, labored to assemble cardboard boxes.

Unlike them, Bly would not be paid—there was no training wage for factory girls in the late nineteenth century.

The women were paid by the box, not by the hour. To earn $1, they needed to complete 200 boxes—which meant handling boxes 1,600 times, as one explained.

"One girl who worked on the floor below me said they were not allowed to tell what they earned," Bly wrote. "However she had been working here five years, and she did not average more than $5 a week. The factory in itself was a totally unfit place for women. The rooms were small and there was no ventilation. In case of fire there was practically no escape."[17]

STUNTS

At her peak, Nellie Bly produced one "stunt" story a week. Biographer Brooke Kroeger explains, "It was not [Bly's] wit or sarcasm or stream-of-consciousness that delivered a ripe audience. It was her compassion and social conscience, buttressed by a disarming bluntness. There was no mind-splitting intellectual insight or noteworthy literary finesse. Bly simply produced, week after week, an uninhibited display of her delight in being female and fearless and her joy in having such an attention-getting place to strut her stuff."[18]

With a stable salary, Bly abandoned her tiny furnished room for sharper digs on the Upper West Side. She began to support her mother, who joined her at 202 West 74th Street. Less than a year later, Bly added newly divorced sister Kate and her daughter Beatrice to the list of her dependents. The quartet settled into a larger apartment on West 37th Street in the fashionable Murray Hill neighborhood.

The fall of 1888 brought national elections. Bly attempted to interview President Grover Cleveland's young wife. A bachelor when he entered the White House, Cleveland had assumed guardianship of his late law partner's young daughter. In 1886, he married her. At 21, Frances Folsom became the youngest first lady in history. Famous for her weekend receptions, which attracted women from

THE TRIANGLE SHIRTWAIST FACTORY FIRE

The doors were locked. It was a Saturday afternoon, on March 25, 1911, when the fire began. The flames quickly spread throughout the eighth and ninth floors of the Triangle Shirtwaist Company. More than 500 women were working for the blouse manufacturer that day.

The year before, strikes against shirtwaist companies represented the first large-scale, female-led labor action. More than 30,000 workers (80 percent of them women) struck companies in Philadelphia and New York. The group failed to get union recognition—male-led unions did not want them. Triangle kept the exit doors locked not only to keep latecomers from working, but also to prevent workers from leaving in mass protest.

Escape was difficult. The first women to reach the locked doors were quickly crushed by those behind them. Others leaped from the windows and the roof, some of them holding hands. They tore through the nets and blankets held by firefighters, crashing onto the pavement. Reporter William Shephard wrote, "The flood of water from the firemen's hoses that ran in the gutter was actually red with blood."*

In less than 20 minutes, 147 women died. Public outcry led to many of the changes demanded by strikers before the tragedy.

---

* Catherine Gourley, *Good Girl Work: Factories, Sweatshops and How Women Changed Their Role in the American Workforce.* Brookfield, Conn.: Millbrook Press, 1991, p. 89.

a variety of backgrounds, she was closemouthed with the media. Bly visited Oak View, the president's private home. Despite her best efforts, she was unable to get an interview.

Firefighters sprayed water on the upper floors of the Asch Building, which housed the Triangle Shirtwaist Company, on March 25, 1911. The fire killed 147 women who were working in unsafe conditions for the blouse manufacturer. Locked doors prevented many from escaping.

She was more successful profiling Belva Lockwood, a woman campaigning for president three decades before her gender could legally vote. An attorney, Lockwood required an act of Congress to be allowed to argue before the U.S. Supreme Court—the first woman to do so. Lockwood told Bly, "Thinking women and working women" supported her desire for men and women to be treated equally. "Society women never go outside society. . . . The very poor—the masses—are no better. One is the slave, and the other the doll and equally useless to us."[19]

Bly's serious profiles alternated with lighter ones. She interviewed champion boxer John L. Sullivan and Laura Dewey Bridgman, who had learned to speak with her fingers and read despite being deaf, mute, and blind. While profiling Bridgman at the Perkins Institution, the director introduced Bly to a nine-year-old girl with similar disabilities and even more remarkable gifts. Her name was Helen Keller.

During her first two years at the *World*, Bly wrote about fraudulent sales of faulty washing machines and the challenges faced by female medical students. She posed as a private investigator and as a woman hoping to purchase a child. She discovered four locations where a newborn could be bought for as little as $10 (less than two weeks' salary).

Bly also pretended to be a criminal. Following her arrest for petty larceny, Bly wrote about being strip-searched by a homeless woman while being spied on by male officers. She was approached by work-seeking attorneys and housed in a coed cell. The men running the jail treated her decently, but Bly believed that women—"matrons"—should be hired for the job. They soon would be.

She interviewed a matron at police headquarters while reporting on how few female criminals reform. Bly had gone undercover so often the matron told her, "I used to wonder what disguise you would come in, but I never thought I would see you as Nellie Bly."[20]

Among her many assignments, Nellie Bly interviewed Belva Lockwood, an attorney who was the first woman to argue before the U.S. Supreme Court. Lockwood also ran for president, 30 years before women were allowed to vote in the United States.

Bly wrote about learning ballet and dancing in a chorus line. Following up on readers' tips, she traveled to New York's capital.

"I went up to Albany to catch a professional briber in the act," she later wrote. "The briber and lobbyist whom I caught was Mr. Ed Phelps. I pretended I wanted to have him kill a certain bill. Mr. Phelps was cautious at first and looked carefully into my record. He satisfied himself that I was honest and talked very freely for a king." [21]

Phelps promised to get the bill killed for $1,000. He would use part of the payment to bribe half a dozen assemblymen.

Bly planned to meet Phelps in a New York hotel room with the money. Instead she wrote her story.

"Her exposure of how legislation is promoted or destroyed was a startling revelation to the Citizens of New York," lauded the *World*. "To Nellie Bly was entrusted the by no means easy task of not only discovering . . . evidence of how bills are killed or forced through the legislature. This mission Nellie Bly undertook and carried through with success at every point." [22]

Phelps disagreed. He claimed to know he was being set up, only offering to bribe state legislators after recognizing Bly.

Bly testified before the Assembly Judiciary Committee. Although her testimony did not lead to any action against the six assemblymen Phelps claimed would accept bribes, the lobbyist quickly left town.

Writing about her testimony, the *Albany Argus* reported,

> She proved to be a slender woman of perhaps 22 or 23 years of age, clad in a dark blue cloth dress with a corsage bouquet of red roses; a somewhat stunning hat with a big gilt arrow at the side crowned a face of some regularity of feature . . . Nellie Bly, or Pink Cochrane as she subsequently announced her

name, evinced an uncontrollable desire to laugh all
through her testimony.[23]

Giggling or not, Bly's fan base increased. So did the
World's circulation. By then many of the *World*'s readers
regularly sought out Bly's byline.

The paper's Sunday edition reached 285,860 copies
on March 25, 1889; by May of that year it reached a daily
average circulation of nearly 350,000. Meanwhile, Bly had
enough fan letters and questions from readers to fill columns when she was not focused on reporting.

Bly's experiences on Blackwell's Island became a best-
selling book, *Ten Days in a Mad-House*. She followed that
success with *Six Months in Mexico*, an account of her experiences in that country that also sold well. Her novel, *The
Mystery of Central Park*, unfortunately, demonstrated that
Bly's talent for reporting facts did not extend to an ability
to write fiction. It failed to attract an audience and earned
poor reviews.

Bly's success was partly due to the way her articles
were enhanced by illustrations. The *World* was a leader in
using pictures to sell newspapers. Accompanying her on
many assignments, celebrated illustrator Walt McDougall
added eye-catching, yet realistic drawings to her articles.
"Nothing was too strenuous nor too perilous for her if it
promised results," he recalled. Bly "suffered the penalty
paid by all sensation-writers of being compelled to hazard
more and more theatric feats."[24]

It was early one morning in the fall of 1888, when she
conceived the idea that topped them all. It would take
another year before she embarked on the story that made
her famous.

The World Takes On Nellie Bly

Nellie Bly was hardly the first person to imagine re-creating Jules Verne's fictional *Around the World in Eighty Days*. Many of the novel's readers considered similar journeys. As travel became increasingly modernized in the decade and a half after the book's publication, the chance of besting the time set by protagonist Phileas Fogg improved.

At the *New York World*, sending a reporter on such a voyage was discussed at an editorial meeting. It was also suggested separately by a reader and several *World* correspondents.

If Bly went, it would do more than determine if an individual could traverse the Earth in under three months. It would also illustrate a single woman's ability to travel unaccompanied in foreign countries during a time when most were chaperoned at home. Bly moved to the top of the list, despite business manager George W. Turner's strenuous objections. While he believed she *would* need a chaperone and too much luggage, she pledged to go alone, and with a single bag.

Fogg's journey was motivated by a bet at a private club. In real life, Henry C. Jarrett accepted a similar wager at New York's Players Club. The recent winner of a trans-continental race, he told the *World* his intentions. Instead of earning notice in the paper, he learned of Bly's proposal. Jarrett bowed out and offered to help Bly plan.

After waiting a year, Nellie Bly had just a few days to get ready. She left Hoboken, New Jersey, on November 14, 1889, at 9:40:30 A.M. aboard the steamship *Augusta Victoria*. A migraine headache sufferer, Bly had not had a single vaca-tion during her time at the *World*. She hoped the journey would provide the rest and relaxation she craved.

The trip had scarcely begun when a fellow passenger asked, "'Do you get seasick?'" Bly remembered, writing, "That was enough; I flew to the railing."

"Sick? I looked blindly down, caring little what the wild waves were saying, and gave vent to my feelings."[1]

Seasick for much of the six-day journey, Bly reached England exhausted. After picking up her messages at the *World*'s offices, she went with the paper's London corre-spondent, Tracey Greaves, to the secretary of the American Legation office. There she received a permanent passport replacing the temporary one given to her by the secretary of state. She also gave her birth date as May 5, 1867—shaving three years off her real age of 25.

From London she caught a train to the English Channel. A boat took her to France and a train traveling from Boulogne to Amiens. The side trip to Amiens cost her a night's sleep. It could also cost her a connection to her

Nellie Bly began her journey around the world on the steamship *Augusta Victoria*, headed from Hoboken, New Jersey, to London. For much of the six days crossing the Atlantic, Bly was seasick.

next ship. Bly took the risk. She could not skip meeting the man who inspired her journey.

THE WRITER, THE MONKEY, AND THE RIVAL

On the Amiens station platform, author Jules Verne waited for Bly alongside his wife and Paris journalist R.H. Sherard. "When I saw them I felt as any other woman would have done under the circumstances," Bly wrote.

> I wondered if my face was travel-stained, and if my hair was tossed. I thought regretfully, had I been traveling on an American train, I should have been able to make my toilet en route, so that when I stepped off at Amiens and faced the famous novelist and his charming wife, I would have been as trim and tidy as I would had I been receiving them in my own home.[2]

At Jules Verne's nearby home, she described her itinerary: "New York to London, then Calais, Brindisi, Port Said, Ismalia, Suez, Aden, Colombo, Penang, Singapore, Hong Kong, Yokohama, San Francisco, New York." Verne asked her why she did not go to Bombay like the hero of his novel. "Because I am more anxious to save time than a young widow," she replied.[3]

Verne's home was considered the finest in the city. Before leaving, Bly asked to see the study where the author worked.

More than 100 years later, an author as famous in this time as Verne was in his offered advice to aspiring writers. "Your writing room doesn't . . . need an Early American roll top desk in which to house your writing implements," Stephen King explained in his book *On Writing*. "I wrote my first two published novels, *Carrie* and *Salem's Lot*, in the laundry room of a doublewide trailer, pounding away on my wife's portable Olivetti typewriter and balancing a child's desk on my thighs; . . . The space can be humble . . . and it really needs only one thing: a door you are willing to shut."[4]

Speeding to her next destination, Bly faced competition. A former reporter for the *New York World*, Elizabeth Bisland, was writing for *Cosmopolitan* magazine when her publisher decided that a race between the two women would be even more newsworthy than Bly's trip alone.

Bisland had less time to prepare than Bly—reportedly less than a day—before taking a train west to San Francisco where she boarded a transpacific ship. Bisland and Bly could cross paths in Hong Kong.

Bly's employer scarcely acknowledged the competition. She might not return with a new philosophy for the meaning of life or a scientific discovery, but the *World* believed her trip was more than a "stunt." She would demonstrate how advanced travel had become in the late nineteenth century. Her trek could be re-created by the average U.S. citizen—albeit one with the money for first-class passage.

A Pittsburgh manufacturer pointed out that a prominent traveler enjoying the usual, leisurely yearlong world tour would have her trip as a guide. Confronted by an emergency, the traveler could refer to the reporter's trek across the planet that "established a standard schedule which may be of inestimable value to many globe trotters or around the world loiterers in the future," he explained.[5]

IN HER OWN WORDS

In her book *Around the World in Seventy-two Days*, Nellie Bly described seeing Jules Verne's study:

> I was astonished. I had expected, judging from the rest of the house, that [Jules] Verne's study would be a room of ample proportions and richly furnished. I had read so many descriptions of the studies of famous authors, and have dwelt with something akin to envy (our space is so limited and expensive in New York) on the ample room, the beautiful hand-carved desks filled with costly trinkets, the rare etchings and paintings that covered the walls, the rich hangings, and, I will confess it, I have thought it small wonder that amid such surroundings authors were able to dream fancies that brought them fame.
>
> But when I stood in M. Verne's study I was speechless. . . . The room was very small; even my little den at home was almost as large. It was also very modest and bare. Before the window was a flat-topped desk. The usual litter that accompanies and fills the desks of most literary persons was conspicuously absent, and the waste-basket that is usually filled to overflowing with what one very

In the beginning, Bly's sightseeing was limited. Her ability to describe London, Greaves pointed out, was "much the same as a man describing Broadway if he were shot through a pneumatic tube from the Western Union building to the 23rd Street Uptown office."[6]

Taking a mail train from Calais, France, to Brindisi, Italy, she skipped Paris by 20 miles (32 kilometers). She never saw much of France. The train's windows were too filthy for decent viewing.

often considers their most brilliant productions, in this case held but a few little scraps.

On the desk was a neat little pile of white paper, probably 8x10 in size. It was part of the manuscript of a novel that M. Verne is engaged on at present. I eagerly accepted the manuscript when he handed it to me, and when I looked at the neat penmanship, so neat in fact that had I not known it was prose I should have thought it was the work of a poet, I was more impressed than ever with the extreme tidiness of this French author. . . .

One bottle of ink and one penholder was all that shared the desk with the manuscript. There was but one chair in the room, and it stood before the desk. The only other piece of furniture was a broad, low couch in the corner, and here in this room with these meager surroundings, Jules Verne has written the books that have brought him everlasting fame.*

---

* Nellie Bly, *Around the World in Seventy-two Days*. New York: Pictorial Weeklies, 1890, pp. 23–24. http://digital.library.upenn.edu/women/bly/world/world.html.

Reaching Italy on November 24, she boarded the *Victoria*, bound for Ismailia, Egypt. Settling in, she asked if there was time for her to leave the ship. If you hurry, she was told.

It was after midnight when a ship's guard led Bly through the dark streets. She woke up the operator at the cable office—where she hoped to send a message via telegraph to the *World*. Unfortunately he did not know where New York City was. Bly wrote that she "explained as best I could; then he brought out a lot of books, through which he searched first, to know by which line he could send the message. . . . The whole thing was so new and amusing to me that I forgot all about the departure of the boat."[7]

"A whistle blew long and warningly. I looked at the guard," Bly remembered, "the guard looked at me. It was too dark to see each other, but I know our faces were the picture of dismay. My heart stopped beating and I thought with emotions akin to horror, 'My boat was gone and with it my limited wardrobe.'

" 'Can you run?' the guard asked in a husky voice. I said I could and he taking a close grasp of my hand, we started down the dark street with a speed that would have startled a deer."[8]

They raced past pedestrians and port security guards. When the two reached the port, they realized the ship they heard whistling was bound for Alexandria. Her ship remained.

All that so she could transmit a short message describing the boring train ride and her exhaustion. The news ran in the *World* on November 26; her letter describing the transatlantic crossing would not appear for nearly two weeks. Mail delivery was far slower than telegraphs, but she could not always find a cable office.

With its star reporter unable to report, the *World* kept its readers' interest by running a contest. The person who came closest to guessing her arrival time would win an all-expenses-paid trip to Europe. Well over a half million entry forms were received.

Bly's later writing detailed her experience on the ships. She described workers scrubbing the deck below and accidentally dousing her bed with water—waking the late sleeper. She complained about the noisy family next to her cabin and the way they interrupted her morning slumber with silly games. Bly told how a man with little money proposed marriage because he mistakenly believed she was an American heiress. Another thought her marriageable, not because of any attraction but because she traveled with a single bag. With his 19 trunks, it seemed like the perfect match.

Both on board ships and at port calls, Bly described the people she encountered. Viewed today, her descriptions seem both insensitive and racist. She called Italians "the poorest and proudest people on earth," complained that her ship was delayed "because some black men had been too slow," and wrote that the beggars outside a Hong Kong temple "were so repulsive that instead of appealing to one's sympathy they only succeed in arousing one's disgust."[9]

In Japan, Bly wrote that "the Japanese are the direct opposite to the Chinese. The Japanese are the cleanliest people on earth, the Chinese are the filthiest; the Japanese are always happy and cheerful, the Chinese are always grumpy and morose; . . . the Japanese have few vices, the Chinese have all the vices in the world; in short, the Japanese are the most delightful of people, the Chinese the most disagreeable."[10]

Bly could be just as critical toward her home country. Writing of traveling in Ceylon (now Sri Lanka), she said that "I have spoken about the perfect roads in Ceylon. I found the roads in the same state of perfection in almost all the Eastern ports at which I stopped. I could not decide, to my own satisfaction, whether the smoothness of the road was due to the entire and blessed absence of beer wagons, or to the absence of the New York street commissioners."[11]

Leaving Europe, she traveled from Ismailia to Aden (now known as Yemen). The intense heat did not discourage Bly from going ashore. She reported on how white the natives' teeth were from cleaning them with a modified toothpick made of tree branches and how men dyed their black hair yellow.

Arriving in Colombo, Ceylon, on December 8, she learned that her next ship—the *Oriental*—would be delayed five days to wait for the mail ship. It could cost her the record. "It is only fair to everybody to state that the elements are against her in that part of the journey where it is most essential that they be propitious [favorable]," the *World* reported.[12]

In Colombo she purchased some rings that were highly prized across the world. After her delay, she sailed to Singapore and purchased something more novel than jewelry.

Reaching her Singapore driver's home, Bly wrote, "At the door of their home was a monkey. I did resist the temptation to buy a boy at Port Said and also smothered the desire to buy a Sinhalese girl at Colombo, but when I saw the monkey my will-power melted and I began straightway to bargain for it. I got it."[13]

FASTER THAN FOGG

"You are going to be beaten." Nellie Bly stared at the ticket agent. She had just arrived in Hong Kong, which she later described as "strangely picturesque . . . a terraced city, the terraces being formed by the castle-like, arcaded buildings perched tier after tier up the mountain's verdant side. The regularity with which the houses are built in rows made me wildly fancy them a gigantic staircase, each stair made in imitation of castles."[14]

Bly was certain the man was wrong. Yet as soon as she told him her name, he had given her the news. "What? I think not. I have made up my delay," she replied.

"You are going to lose it," he told her. She knew he had to be wrong and asked him what he meant. "Aren't you having a race around the world?" he asked her.

"Yes; quite right," she replied. "I am running a race with Time."

"Time? I don't think that's her name."[15]

Thirty-nine days into her trip, Bly learned about Bisland. Her rival had left three days before; Bly was going to be delayed another five.

Bisland had told the agent that her race was arranged by the *World.* Bly had no way of knowing that Bisland was not working for the newspaper. Yet she refused to be discouraged. She was racing against Phileas Fogg after all, not Bisland.

"I promised my editor that I would go around the world in seventy-five days, and if I accomplish that I shall be satisfied," she explained. "I am not racing with anyone. I would not race. If someone else wants to do the trip in less time, that is their concern. . . . I promised to do the trip in seventy-five days, and I will do it; although had I been permitted to make the trip when I first proposed it over a year ago, I should then have done it in sixty days."[16]

Bly spent her time in Hong Kong refusing social events—she lacked the right clothes—and visiting mainland China. Her descriptions of the country's method for executing prisoners were especially vivid.

"I was very anxious to see the execution ground, so we were carried there [on chairs attached to poles operated by several Chinese]," Bly wrote.

> I noticed the ground in one place was very red, and when I asked Ah Cum [her guide] about it he said indifferently, as he kicked the red-colored earth

with his white-soled shoe: "It's blood. Eleven men were beheaded here yesterday. . . . When women are condemned to death in China they are bound to wooden crosses and cut to pieces. . . . Men are beheaded with one stroke unless they are the worst kind of criminals."[17]

There was more to come. Bly saw the heads of the executed, preserved in lime. She visited prison cells featuring open doors and narrow doorways. When she saw "the prisoners with thick, heavy boards fastened about their necks, I no longer felt surprised at the doors being unbarred. There was no need of locking them." She described examining "split bamboo to whip with, thumb screws, pulleys on which people are hanged by their thumbs, and such pleasant things. Sticking bamboo splints under the finger nails and then setting fire to them is another happy way of punishing wrongdoers," along with "being whipped, ground to death, boiled in oil, beheaded, put under red hot bells, being sawed in twain, and undergoing similar agreeable things."[18]

On December 28, the *Oceanic* left Hong Kong, reaching Yokohama, Japan, five days later. Nellie Bly spent New Year's Eve at sea.

In Japan, she wrote about visiting a house to "see the dancing, or *geisha*, girls. At the door we saw all the wooden shoes of the household, and we were asked to take off our shoes before entering, a proceeding rather disliked by some of the party, who refused absolutely to do as requested. We affected a compromise, however, by putting cloth slippers over our shoes."[19]

Upon being entertained by the geishas, Bly wrote, "The Japanese are the only women I ever saw who could rouge and powder and be not repulsive, but the more charming because of it. They powder their faces and have a way of reddening their under lip just at the tip that gives them

While in Japan, Nellie Bly visited a geisha house, though some in her party balked at taking off their shoes before entering. The Japanese left Bly with a much more favorable impression than the Chinese did.

a most tempting look. The lips look like two luxurious cherries."[20]

During her stay, a Japanese reporter interviewed her. The interest from the foreign press was merely a hint of things to come.

On January 11, she boarded the *Oceanic*, now bound for the United States and the Port of San Francisco. It was the vessel she had taken from Hong Kong, with one difference. Inscribed upon the ship engines was this message: "For Nellie Bly; We'll win or die; January 20, 1890." [21]

HOME

Writing later, Bly reported that on the third day "a storm came upon us. . . . and it continued, never abating a moment; head winds, head sea, wild rolling, frightful pitching, until I fretfully waited for noon when I would slip off to the dining-room to see the run, hoping that it would have gained a few miles on the day before, and always being disappointed." Everyone tried to cheer her, but Bly's mood turned dark. " 'If I fail, I will never return to New York,' I would say despondently; 'I would rather go in dead and successful than alive and behind time.' "[22]

Bly had traveled more than 21,000 miles (33,800 kilometers) in 67 days. She learned that some crew members blamed the storm on a "Jonah," the biblical figure whose responsibility for a similar storm led to him being thrown overboard and subsequently swallowed by a waiting fish.

> I was told that the sailors said monkeys were Jonahs. Monkeys brought bad weather to ships, and as long as the monkey was on board we would have storms. Someone asked if I would consent to [my] monkey being thrown overboard. . . . Just then someone told me that ministers were Jonahs; they always brought bad weather to ships. We had two ministers on board! So I said quietly, if the ministers were thrown overboard I'd say nothing about the monkey. Thus the monkey's life was saved.[23]

Nellie Bly and her monkey saw the shoreline on January 20. "A hopefulness that had not known me for many days came back," she wrote, "when in rushed the purser, his face a snow-white, crying: 'My God, the bill of health was left behind in Yokohama.' " Asking what that meant, Bly learned that without a bill of health the ship would not be allowed to land until another ship arrived from Japan—in two weeks. "I would cut my throat, for I could not live and endure it," Bly threatened.[24]

The bill was uncovered inside the ship doctor's desk. Bly's stress continued.

A small tug was hired for her. "There was no time for farewells," Bly admitted. "The monkey was taken on the tug with me, and my baggage, which had increased by gifts from friends, was thrown after me. Just as the tug steamed off the quarantine doctor called to me that he had forgotten to examine my tongue, and I could not land until he did. I stuck it out, he called out 'all right' [and] the others laughed."[25]

The tug opposed the *World*'s original premise that Bly's journey be one an average citizen could re-create. The first part of her trek across the United States was equally assisted. A tremendous snowstorm blocked passage across the Sierra Nevada mountain ranges. A single rail car powered by a single engine was hired for Bly. It sped toward Chicago, avoiding the impassable southern route. In Illinois, she joined regular passengers heading east upon the Pennsylvania Railroad.

In the late 1800s, presidents and presidential candidates often made speeches from the backs of trains. The crowds that greeted Bly rivaled any of these "whistle stops." In Columbus, Ohio, the station manager claimed the crowds cheering Bly outnumbered ones for Presidents Cleveland or Harrison. Half of them were women.

When she reached the city where her career began—Pittsburgh—even her 3:10 A.M. arrival did not deter the crowds. In Philadelphia they numbered more than 5,000.

Bly made the cross-country trek in four-and-a-half days. A slow excursion compared to twenty-first century airline travel, it still compares favorably to modern train, bus, or car trips from Northern California to New Jersey.

New York's own F.W. Stevens submitted the winning guess to the *World*. Bly's total time: 72 days, 6 hours, 11 minutes, and 15 seconds. Having spent much of her rail journey dictating to a stenographer, Bly's story ran the day after her arrival—a Sunday.

Despite beating the fictional Fogg and the real-life Bisland (whose transatlantic passage was slowed by storms),

PRESENTING THE GLOBE-GIRDLER A GOLDEN GLOBE. THE ARRIVAL IN PHILADELPHIA.

AROUND THE WORLD IN SEVENTY-TWO DAYS AND SIX HOURS—RECEPTION OF NELLIE BLY AT JERSEY CITY ON THE COMPLETION OF HER JOURNEY—From Sketches by C Bunnell.—[See Page 7.]

Crowds congratulated Nellie Bly upon her arrival in Jersey City as she completed her round-the-world trip. Traveling the last leg across the United States by train, scores of people turned out to see her, as shown in the inset picture of her arrival in Philadelphia.

Bly did not recommend that her fellow citizens undertake similar journeys. "There is really not much for Americans to see in the foreign lands," she told a reporter for the *Topeka Daily Capital*.

We've got the best of everything here; we lack in nothing; then when you go over there you must be robbed, you get nothing to eat and you see nothing that America cannot improve upon wonderfully. There is a great deal more to see at home than abroad. They are so very, very slow in Europe and to my mind are behind America in almost everything.[26]

For Richer
or Poorer

Nellie Bly was the most famous woman in the world. Returning to New York, she discovered her life was radically altered. Named after a song, Bly and her trip inspired their own popular hit. Advertisers clamored for Bly's image just as they do for championship athletes in the twenty-first century. Her face advertised Schenk's Mandrake Pills. The "Nellie Bly" style of cap—resembling the one she wore on her trip around the world—became a huge seller. And a board game based upon her journey appeared in the February 26, 1890, edition of the *World* before being manufactured by McLoughlin Brothers for several decades.

To raise money for the Washington Memorial Arch on Fifth Avenue, Bly's photograph was sold as a collectible.

One hundred photos were priced at $5 each—a week's wage for the average factory girl. They sold out. Bly also profited: Accepting a series of paid lecture dates, she earned nearly $10,000.

Still, the one place she expected to receive the most gave her the least. Her trip around the world helped the *New York World* sell newspapers. The Sunday edition published the day after her return broke circulation records. The *World*'s circulation continued to rise. The paper ran articles related to the trip for months afterward.

She had received a bonus after Blackwell's Island. This time, she did not.

"[*World* publisher Joseph] Pulitzer cabled his congratulations," Bly wrote travel writer Frank G. Carpenter, "and begged me to accept a gift he was sending from India. I accepted the congratulations but have never seen the present." She explained that some in the office claimed to have had a medal struck in her honor, but "I have it on good authority that medal was given as a prize in a telegrapher's contest."[1]

This reaction might have been because of a story she had written. The October 29, 1889, *World* described Bly's efforts to find a cure for her migraines. Visiting seven different doctors, she received seven different diagnoses and seven different "cures." The lack of consensus led her to question the doctors' abilities.

The doctors threatened to sue, claiming the reporter had published false statements that harmed their reputations. Biographer Brooke Kroeger could not find any documents relating to such a suit but feels the threat of a libel action "hurled at the newspaper in the midst of [Bly's] triumphant world journey" meant that "Pulitzer might have been put off [by] the idea of offering her the kind of bonus which would have been within reason for her to expect. Although Bly's own version of why she broke with

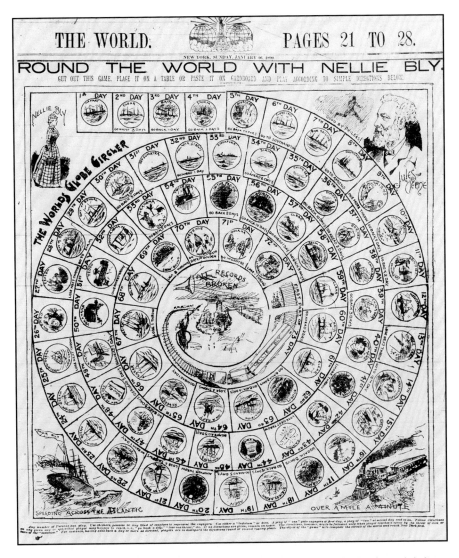

Nellie Bly returned from her around-the-world adventure more of a celebrity than she had ever been. Advertisers used her image in their campaigns, and the *New York World* put out this board game based on her travels.

the *World* makes no mention of her embarrassing legal wrangle, she wasn't in the habit of disclosing embarrassing details about herself."[2]

Bly took a vacation from the *World* in February 1890. Her newspaper promised the reporter's return following her lecture tour. Instead, she left for three years. Nellie Bly planned to become a novelist.

FAIRLY FICTION

When Bly left the *World*, the editor who hired her, Colonel John Cockerill, was earning more than $10,000 a year. The income would have been sufficient to purchase a large house, every year, with money left over for expenses. He was one of the highest-paid newspaper editors in the country. Nellie Bly outearned him her second year as a novelist.

Hired by N.L. Frank Munro, the publisher of the *New York Family Story Paper*, Bly received a three-year contract for contributing fiction in serial installments. It guaranteed her $10,000 the first year and $15,000 for the next two. It was how many successful novelists began, including Charles Dickens.

After Bly signed the contract, her mother signed a five-year lease on a farm in White Plains, New York. Nellie Bly, her mother, her monkey, and her dog left the city for the countryside. *Around the World in Seventy-two Days*, Bly's account of her record-breaking trip, was already a best-seller. Now she looked forward to writing from home without the challenges of reporting. There was only one problem. She could not write fiction.

Few writers are equally successful at nonfiction and fiction. Using her unique point of view and homey writing style, Bly reported unfamiliar experiences and situations. Creating stories from her imagination—especially on a regular basis—was far more difficult. She asked friends for help developing storylines. Illustrator Walt McDougall, who accompanied her on many of her articles, suggested having the main character fall into a rattlesnake pit. After that, Bly could spend each week getting the protagonist in and out of death-defying challenges.

She was unsuccessful. Confined to crutches for an unnamed injury, isolated from her friends, and with the white-hot light of fame quickly fading, she slid into "the most frightening depression that can beset a mortal."[3]

Other than her failed novel, there is no known record of her fiction. Despite extensive searching, Bly biographer Brooke Kroeger was unable to locate any issues of *Family Story* containing Bly's work.

Three years after her departure, the *World* celebrated Pulitzer's decade-long ownership with a 100-page edition. Published on May 10, 1893, it included a 10-page, 10-year synopsis highlighting significant stories. Just a single reporter's name appeared. Featured on three of those pages was the name Nellie Bly.

THE REAL *WORLD*

"[Nellie Bly] has not been in a convent during the last three years," reported the trade paper the *Journalist*, "but only in a strange garret. When through her indomitable pluck with the assistance of the *World*, she awoke to find herself famous, she forgot that her successes were only in doing odd little things and that literary merit had little to do with them. . . . Now she comes back to the *World* to make her name again."[4]

The *World* and the world had both changed. Cockerill had quit—frustrated by Pulitzer's micromanagement and contradicting directives. His replacement, Morrill Goddard, was a graduate of Ivy League Dartmouth College who made the paper even more sensationalized. Goddard asked Bly to come back.

"Stunt reporting" by then had become more about the "stunt" and less about the "reporting." Its popularity waned. Since its practitioners were often women, its declining popularity meant a decline in women reporters as "hard news" front-page reporters. Those who did not quit were shunted to the women's pages.

Not Nellie Bly. Her return was trumpeted with a front-page headline. "Nellie Bly Again," promised the column on the left-hand side, above the fold. Her name was above the headline describing the article.

"More than a half-century later," Kroeger explained, "leading women reporters would still be complaining about the editorial barrier that kept them from 'making the front page.' Bly managed to repeatedly violate this unwritten restriction. Unfortunately for her female successors, she had not unbolted the shackles of gender, she had only slipped through them."[5]

Her return to reporting when "stunts" were disfavored scarcely affected her. After all, Kroeger notes, "Bly did not set up fishing expeditions for scandal. . . . Instead, she targeted specific situations or individuals in an effort to right wrongs, to explain the unexplored, to satisfy curiosity about the intriguing, to expose unfairness, or to catch a thief."[6]

The newsroom was not the only thing altered during Bly's absence. The outside world was also changed.

TAKING ON THE WORLD

Bly's articles reflected the times. For the article marking her return, she interviewed anarchist Emma Goldman.

Jailed for incitement to riot, 25-year-old Goldman received a sympathetic portrait. Bly described Goldman as "the little anarchist, the modern Joan of Arc . . . a little bit of a girl, just five feet high . . . not showing her 120 pounds with a saucy, turned-up nose and very expressive blue-gray eyes that gazed inquiringly at me through shell-rimmed glasses."[7]

Bly included Goldman's views on marriage (she was against it) and murder for political purposes (generally against it as well). Although she wanted to see the government overthrown, Goldman proclaimed her innocence. Eventually convicted and sentenced to a year in prison, she did her time at the jail on Blackwell's Island.

Other articles were similarly informed by current events. Bly traveled to Saratoga for the State Democratic Convention and Chicago to cover the Pullman strike.

In the 1890s, unions—groups of workers united for common goals like higher wages and improved working conditions—were gaining power. From 1881 to 1890, the Bureau of Statistics estimated that workers participated in nearly 10,000 strikes and lockouts.

THE PANIC OF '93

Throughout the 1880s, the U.S. economy benefited from advances in technology and the availability of money at low interest rates. Railroads expanded, businesses hired new employees, and wages grew. In 1893, that changed.

Easy credit fed the expansion of the 1880s. In the 1890s, businesses defaulted on loans and banks tightened lending.

On June 15, 1893, short-term interest rates rose to as high as 75 percent. Unable to get loans, businesses began to fail. In the United States, some one-third of all railroads and 16,000 businesses failed. Over the next four years, immigration declined by four-fifths. In New York nearly 100,000 people lost their jobs, and 20,000 lost their homes. Like the Great Depression 40 years later, breadlines formed in cities across the country. The *World* did its part by starting its own bread fund to help the hungry of New York.

Striking workers from the Pullman Company, a manufacturer of sleeping berths for railroad cars, were supported by other railroad employees. Trains were idled. President Grover Cleveland sent out federal forces, because mail delivery was impacted.

The Pullman workers struck after the economic crisis reduced train orders. George M. Pullman laid off half the workers and cut wages by 25 percent for the rest. Anticipating labor unrest, Pullman had constructed a town where his workers were required to live. "We are born in a Pullman house," explained one worker, "fed from the Pullman shops, taught in the Pullman school, catechized in the Pullman church and when we die we go to the Pullman hell."[8]

Despite the workers' pay cut, the rent and utilities they paid to the Pullman Company remained the same. The rent was deducted from their paychecks and averaged 25 percent more than the rent in nearby communities.

Traveling to Illinois, "so far as I understood the question, I thought the inhabitant of the model town of Pullman hadn't a reason on earth to complain," Bly wrote. "With this belief I visited the town, intending in my article to denounce the rioters and bloodthirsty strikers. . . . Before I had been half a day in Pullman, I was the most bitter striker in the town."[9]

Bly's opinion changed after she witnessed the workers' poor living conditions. Her article offered sympathetic coverage of the strikers and less flattering portraits of the governor of Illinois and Pullman himself. Pulitzer had fired an editor whose editorial supported the strike, yet Bly's article did not cause her any problem. When Governor John Altgeld of Illinois suggested that Pulitzer would not publish her pro-striker article, Bly explained, "It's already been printed. . . . [Pulitzer employed] people to find out and publish the truth about everything, regardless of all other considerations, and if the truth is not given it is solely the fault of the writer, not the paper."[10]

Despite getting away with more, she could not avoid landing unappealing assignments. For every hard-hitting news story, Bly was obligated to author a light feature. For every interview she conducted with an imprisoned murderer, she had to profile a society matron. By 1895, Bly had had enough. She accepted a job in Chicago writing for the *Chicago Herald*.

The job only lasted five weeks. Nellie Bly was getting married.

MR. AND MRS. NELLIE BLY

The *Town Tattler* suggested that Nellie Bly was really undercover, preparing to write about the end of her fake marriage. Bly was indeed married, but it was not a stunt.

She met Robert Seaman on a train, or at a dance, depending upon the source. What is not disputed is that they met, courted, and married within a fortnight. Seaman was 70 years old. He was also a millionaire.

Some biographers suggest that, at 31, Bly had finally found both security and a father figure—replacing the one she had lost as a girl. Never married, Seaman may have considered her more marriageable than most men her own age would have.

The *World* announced her marriage beneath the headline: "Mr. and Mrs. Nellie Bly," assuring readers that "few women have had more world experience at the age of thirty than Miss Bly and few are more capable of enjoying the pleasures of 'a millionaire existence.'"[11]

Walt McDougall believed that Bly quit the *World* not from unhappiness with the work but from a broken heart. For years she had been romantically linked to *Life* magazine's drama critic, James Stetson Metcalfe. By early

1895, he was engaged to another. For Bly, Seaman may have seemed like the best, last chance.

It would be expected in the 1890s that she would stop working and devote her life to taking care of her husband. Bly rarely did the expected.

Seaman owned the Iron Clad Manufacturing Company in New York, which manufactured metal containers. He had a large home on Murray Hill along with real estate in several New York counties. His unmarried siblings worried that Bly was after his money. In the beginning, he did not trust her either.

Seaman had private detectives follow Bly and Metcalfe, suspecting they were still involved. Bly was outraged. She had the detectives arrested.

Perhaps encouraged by his worried siblings, on December 24, 1895, Seaman drew up a will leaving Bly a mere $300 (although she was also entitled to the widow's third). Unhappy with *that* Christmas present, Bly went back to the *World*.

Goddard left soon after her return. He was replaced by Arthur Brisbane, a longtime Bly admirer. Her assignments improved, including an interview with the legendary Susan B. Anthony, at the National Woman Suffrage Convention. Bly wrote critically of the women fighting for their right to vote, upset not by their politics but their attire. "I never could see any reason for a woman to neglect her appearance merely because she is intellectually inclined," Bly wrote. "In working for a cause I think it is wise to show some men that its influence does not make women any the less attractive."[12]

Anthony, on the other hand, struck Bly as quite stylish. In her seventies and never married, she told Bly, "I never felt that I could give up my life of freedom to become a man's housekeeper. When I was young, [if a girl married] wealth, she became a pet and a doll."[13]

Returning to work at the *New York World* in early 1896, Nellie Bly interviewed women's rights activist Susan B. Anthony. She was impressed by Anthony's style but did not always have kind remarks for women suffragists, wondering why they seemed to neglect their appearance.

Although Bly did not want to be a man's doll, Seaman did not want to lose her. In August 1896, he took her to Europe, along with her mother, her sister Kate, and Kate's daughter Beatrice. It would be a more luxurious and leisurely trip than the one she took for the *World*. In November, he drew up another will. Bly was named executrix of his estate and rewarded handsomely.

For a time, life was idyllic. Then in the summer of 1899, Kate contracted tuberculosis and died. Bly sought a way to overcome her grief. She did not return to writing. Instead, "purely as a mental distraction," she began to work in her husband's company.[14]

Seaman's company was losing money. In 1899, he hired a new general manager, Major Edward R. Gilman, a West Point graduate who had made more than $150,000 on Wall Street the year before.

In 1904, Seaman was crossing the street when he was hit by a horse-drawn carriage. He died soon after.

According to Bly, at the time of her husband's death, she had taken a company that was $300,000 in debt and not only retired the debt but also increased its sales to more than $1 million a year with profits around $200,000. Along with Gilman, she started a separate company, the American Steel Barrel Company, to sell the barrels she had invented. By 1905, Bly had 25 patents, many on products her late husband's company now manufactured.

Witnessing the deprivations of workers as a reporter, Bly did all she could to ensure that her employees were treated well. No one was paid by the piece; they were guaranteed a wage. Resembling a 2000-era Internet start-up more than an early twentieth-century manufacturing plant, the workers enjoyed a gymnasium, a bowling alley, and a 5,000-volume library. She had a health center built on-site, and sick employees could request a doctor. They were charged 50 cents for the house call, with the rest covered by the company.

Focused on the well-being of the workers and the sales of her product, Bly neglected the bottom line. Accountants she hired slowly stole from the company—several million dollars over the course of a few years. Although Bly discovered Gilman was responsible for a fraudulent business transaction worth $50,000, she forgave him. By then the two may have been romantically involved—another reason Bly ignored her company's creeping debt.

The company was not paying its bills. After Gilman's death in 1910 from stomach cancer, Bly uncovered the fraud committed by the company's chief cashier, Charles Caccia, and assistant cashier, Stanley Gielnik. Caccia and Gielnik both forged checks, cashing them at numerous banks in which the company did not have accounts.

"While I do not believe that [Gilman] was a member of the conspiracy to loot the Iron Clad, his dishonesty made that conspiracy possible," Bly later admitted. Forced into bankruptcy, Bly spent much of her time convincing the court that Iron Clad was separate from the American Steel Barrel Company. She hoped to keep the business she had begun, even if her husband's was eventually dissolved.[15]

She wrote her last editor at the *World*, Arthur Brisbane, asking for his advice and financial help. By then he had left the *World* and gone to work for a publisher every bit as daring and rich as Joseph Pulitzer.

William Randolph Hearst began his journalism career as a reporter for the *World*. Using family money, he purchased a number of newspapers across the country, imitating the Pulitzer style. To staff the *New York Evening Journal*, Hearst hired Goddard and his entire staff of editors and reporters at double their salary. He even stole the *World*'s popular comic strip, *The Yellow Kid*. After Pulitzer retaliated by publishing a similar-shaded comic strip, the rivals' competition became known as "yellow journalism."

Hearst hired Brisbane to work directly under him, running the day-to-day operations of his publications. With his

Arthur Brisbane, Nellie Bly's former editor at the *New York World*, was working for publisher William Randolph Hearst at the *New York Evening Journal* in 1912. Brisbane persuaded Bly to return to reporting and work for him at the *Evening Journal*.

salary tied to circulation growth, he was earning more than $250,000 a year by the early 1900s.

In 1912, Brisbane had a suggestion for Bly. He believed that her talent lay not in business but in reporting, "doing much more useful work than making tin cans," he explained. "Being tied to a factory and a lot of scoundrels cannot have been such very great happiness." If Bly was worried about money, then she should work for him.[16]

Bly began reporting for the *New York Evening Journal*, covering that year's Republican and Democratic Conventions. She also wrote about demonstrations by women in Washington, D.C., demanding the right to vote. This time, she noted, many were better dressed.

In 1914, Bly needed a vacation. She planned to meet with an Austrian investor who might save the American Steel Barrel Company. The reporter could not have picked a worse time to visit Europe.

10

"The Best Reporter in America"

Nellie Bly boarded the RMS *Oceanic* on August 1, 1914. The ship was bound for Southampton, England; Bly was bound for Vienna, Austria. Just four days before, Austria had declared war on Serbia while Germany invaded Luxembourg. So, the ship's crossing was stressful for most of the passengers. Not for Bly.

During the trip, Bly wrote a letter to her mother admitting, "There is no telling where we shall land, or if I ever shall get to Vienna." There were rumors that the ship's cargo included $4 million in gold. Some passengers believed that the Germans would intercept the vessel and steal the gold. "I hope they do," Bly confessed. She had found the trip boring, with the various nationalities unwilling to interact with non-countrymen—"They all seem afraid of each other," Bly noted.[1]

Bly reached Vienna on August 11. In Paris, she had received an emergency passport, lying when she gave Switzerland as her destination.

Bly was not in Europe to report on the war. She was there to meet with Oscar Bondy, a wealthy Austrian. She planned to sign the American Steel Barrel Company over to him, hoping to prevent its seizure for debts incurred by her late husband's businesses. Still, Bly was a reporter. A U.S. military report later described Bly's desire to report from the front lines "and that she did not mind at all whether or not she was killed because of her discouragement over her financial affairs in this country previous to her departure."[2]

From 1914 until early 1919, Bly lived in Vienna with occasional trips to Germany and Switzerland. She avoided returning to New York and its bankruptcy courts, creditors, and bad debts. The choice to stay in Europe gave her a unique vantage point. In the early stages of the war, she was one of the few U.S. reporters covering the battles along the Eastern Front. She traveled to the battlefields, where shells were lobbed less than 100 yards (91 meters) from her position. She visited the crude hospitals on the periphery of warfare and described the horrific injuries she observed. Watching a Russian soldier dying at a hospital in Budapest, she learned that he was asking for his children. In the *New York Evening Journal* she wrote of asking the man's doctor, "Could Emperors and Czars and Kings look on this torturing slaughter and ever sleep again?" Bly recorded his response: "'They do not look,' he said gently."[3]

Bly was not the only female reporter during World War I. In 1918, Elizabeth Shepley Sergeant began to

WAR!

The war began with an assassination. On June 28, 1914, a Bosnian Serb nationalist assassinated Archduke Franz Ferdinand, heir to the throne of Austria-Hungary. Under Kaiser Wilhelm, Germany had built up its military so that "the Germans were prepared, at the very least, to run the risk of causing a large-scale war," explains Dr. Gary Sheffield, a professor at King's College London. "The crumbling Austro-Hungarian Empire decided, after the assassination on 28 June, to take action against Serbia, which was suspected of being behind the murder. The German government issued the so-called 'blank check' on 5-6 July, offering unconditional support to the Austrians, despite the risk of war with Russia. . . . A wish to unite the nation behind the government may have been a motive. So might desire to strike against Russia before it had finished rebuilding its military strength after its defeat by Japan in 1905."*

Germany soon invaded Luxembourg, Belgium, and France, while its ally Austria-Hungary invaded Serbia. Along the Eastern Front, the Russian army was successful in its fight with the Austro-Hungarians but was less successful against the Germans. Although Germany's march to Paris was halted, the Western Front settled into static but devastating trench warfare. "The Great War," later known as World War I, eventually involved more than 70 million military personnel, 60 million of them European. Some 15 million people died. For that reason it was often called "The War to End All Wars" until World War II, two decades later, cost even more lives.

---

* Gary Sheffield, "The Origins of World War One," BBC History. November 5, 2009. http://www.bbc.co.uk/history/worldwars/wwone/origins_01.shtml.

In this photograph from 1916, German soldiers fought from the trenches on the Eastern Front during World War I. Nellie Bly was one of the few U.S. journalists to report from the battlefields on the Eastern Front.

work as a war correspondent covering the Western Front for the *New Republic* until she was injured by a grenade.

Besides her regular, front-page contributions to the *New York Evening Journal*, Bly contributed stories locally. Reading her article in the Vienna newspaper, *Die Zeit*, Bly was upset by how severely edited her article was. Her story contained little information of military value, so she did not understand why government censors exorcised so much. The Foreign Ministry's press chief, Oskar von Montlong, explained that it was not the military but the paper's editors who cut the sections, because Bly's piece opposed the paper's liberal viewpoint. "I apologize for my unjust suspicions of the censors. . . . I have heard such things happened occasionally in America, but never to me," she wrote to von Montlong. "Fortunately my articles are always printed as I write them, whether they coincide with the editorial opinion or not."[4]

Bly's own opinion would soon be suspect. Isolated by her location, she seemed unaware of public opinion back home. Fiercely anti-British—as many in the United States were in the early 1900s—Bly supported the Austrians and their German allies. A majority of her fellow citizens also opposed U.S. involvement in the war. Indeed, Woodrow Wilson was reelected president in 1916 partly on the strength of his campaign slogan: He kept us out of war.

On May 7, 1915, a German submarine launched two torpedoes at the civilian British Cunard liner *Lusitania*. It sank in 18 minutes, taking to their deaths some 1,198 passengers—most of them women and children. Among the dead were 128 Americans.

Nearly two years later, decoded messages from Germany revealed its attempts to involve Mexico in the conflict. Germany promised assistance if the United States' southern neighbor invaded, helping Mexico to get Texas, Arizona, and New Mexico back.

On noon, April 6, 1917, Wilson finally declared war. Bly's situation was precarious. She wrote little. Instead, she focused her attention on getting contributions for Austrian widows and orphans. Technically an enemy alien (as her country was fighting Austria), she was able to go about her days unharmed, even wearing an American flag lapel pin.

With the addition of U.S. soldiers and armaments, the war's course changed. By late 1918 it was over. It was time for Nellie Bly to come home.

RETURN

After the United States' declaration of war, Oscar Bondy became an enemy alien. Transferring the company to

Bondy kept it out of bankruptcy court but moved it instead to the Alien Property Custodian. Back home in the United States, Bly's mother filed suit to have the business returned to her control.

In February 1920, U.S. District Judge Edwin L. Garvin ruled that Nellie Bly and not her mother was the rightful owner of the company. According to biographer Brooke Kroeger, "Garvin said so much bitterness between the parties surrounded the case that the court had made every effort to reconcile their conflicting interests 'and to restore the natural relation of mother and daughter.' That proved impossible, he said."[5]

The business was ended by debt, and Bly's relationship with her mother—whom she had supported financially most of her adult life—ended as well. In her 50s, and broke, Nellie Bly needed a job.

She returned to the *New York Evening Journal*, pursuing a different kind of reporting. Writing as Margery Rex, Julia McCarthy was the paper's Bly-like front-page reporter, covering kidnappings and scandals.

Instead, Bly worked as an advice columnist. She championed local labor, demanding American shippers hire American. When unemployed men and women wrote to her, she helped them find work. Most of all, she found homes for the children of unwed mothers, acting as her own adoption agency. Operating from her room at the McAlpin Hotel, Bly placed hundreds of children and devoted as much time to finding suitable homes for them as she did writing her columns.

Driven to help as many children as she could (and report her successes), Bly neglected her health. Suffering from bronchopneumonia, the reporter entered St. Mark's Hospital on January 9, 1922. That day her last article appeared in the *Journal*. She died a little more than two weeks later, on January 27.

After returning to the United States following World War I, Nellie Bly wrote an advice column for the *New York Evening Journal*. She spent much of her time trying to find homes for the children of unwed mothers.

"Nellie Bly was THE BEST REPORTER IN AMERICA," Arthur Brisbane wrote the next day, "and that is saying a great deal. Reporting requires intelligence, precision, honesty of purpose and accuracy. . . . Nellie Bly died too young, cheated of the fortune that should have been her own, suffering for years from ill health that could not diminish her courage or her kindness of heart."[6]

LEGACY

During Nellie Bly's last years at the *New York Evening Journal*, the role of female reporters had already changed. When she began her career, most women journalists were confined to "the women's page." At the *New York World*, Joseph Pulitzer's policy of hiring talented people and putting them in competition with one another did not spare Bly. While Bly was the best known, at 23 Elizabeth Jordan reported for the *World* about prisons and spent a night in an all-male mining camp armed with a knife. In 1892, Jordan became the assistant Sunday editor.

Fearing that other stunt reporters could become as famous—and as expensive—as Bly, Pulitzer employed a number of women under a shared byline: Meg Merrilies. These anonymous writers posed as inmates, leaped in front of trolley cars, and tested an early bulletproof vest (by being shot at).

Despite her successes, by the time Bly was working in the 1920s, she was seen less as a role model than as a relic. She came from a time of corsets and clear divisions between the sexes. The young female reporters she met were allowed to vote. They smoked and went to bars and had abandoned corsets, wearing dresses that flapped when they danced (thus the name flappers.)

Unemployment from the Great Depression reduced their ranks. Publishers were more likely to employ a man with a family to support. Partly inspired by her close friend, Associated Press reporter Lorena Hickok, First Lady Eleanor Roosevelt instituted a once-a-week, "women-only" press conference at the White House. This forced news organizations to employ at least one female reporter. Meanwhile, popular movies like 1931's *The Front Page* and 1940's *His Girl Friday* depicted hard-driving, tough-talking female reporters.

In the 1940s, World War II offered unprecedented opportunities for female journalists. By the end of the war, some 127 women had secured official military accreditation as war correspondents. Martha Gellhorn, who was married to Ernest Hemingway during her time reporting on World War II, covered every major war from the Spanish Civil War to the Cold War's conclusion. In 1944, Marguerite Higgins was a war correspondent in Europe for the *New York Herald Tribune*. Six years later, she became chief of the paper's Tokyo bureau. May Craig best summed up the achievements of female reporters in a 1944 speech at the Women's National Press Club: "The war has given women a chance to show what they can do in the news world, and they have done well."[7]

Reporting in the middle of the twentieth century, Ethel Payne was soon called the "first lady of the black press." Covering the U.S. civil rights movement, she was the first African-American commentator to join a national television network.

Had Bly come of age in the twenty-first century, she might well have been a television reporter. Her early "stunt reporting" resembled the undercover investigative work highlighted on network newsmagazines like *60 Minutes*, while her good looks and vibrant personality might have given her anchor opportunities. Today some of the highest-paid and best-known newscasters on television are women. From Barbara Walters, the first woman to anchor the evening news for a major network, to Katie Couric, who served as anchor and managing editor for the *CBS Evening News*, a number of female broadcasters have commanded multimillion-dollar salaries over the past 30 years.

Despite the shining stars, inequalities continue to exist. The 2009 Media Report to Women notes that the percentage of women working in daily newsrooms stands at 37.58 percent, while 64.8 percent of supervisors are male, along with 58.2 percent of copy editors, 60.9 percent of reporters and 72.9 percent of photographers. This despite the fact that women have represented the majority of journalism majors since 1977 and are more likely to find full-time employment after graduation than their male counterparts.

Today, employment concerns affect both sexes. Newspaper circulations are declining, while Internet news sites rarely charge for their content. As a result, staff and salaries have been reduced at newspapers while budgets for most television news departments have also declined.

Addressing the Class of 2009 at the University of California, Berkeley, Graduate School of Journalism, author and journalist Barbara Ehrenreich spoke to both men and women when she explained that, being a reporter in the twenty-first century, "you won't get rich. . . . You'll be living some of the problems you report on. . . . You might never have a cleaning lady. In fact you might be one. I can't tell you how many writers I know who have moonlighted as cleaning ladies or waitresses. . . .

"We are not part of the elite. We are part of the working class, which is exactly how journalists have seen themselves through most of American history—as working stiffs."[8]

When Joseph Pulitzer purchased the *New York World*, he told his staff, "You have all been living in the parlor and taking baths every day. Now you are all walking down the Bowery."[9]

Pulitzer did not plan to cut his reporters' pay. Instead, he wanted them to write stories about the lives of the poor and the working class. These were the stories at which Nellie Bly excelled.

Yet in the decades following her death, interest in Bly faded. In 1986, journalist Brooke Kroeger wanted to explain to her 10-year-old daughter, Brett, why they lived as they did. The family moved often, living in foreign cities like Brussels and Tel Aviv while Kroeger pursued her reporting dreams, dreams inspired by Bly.

Disappointed by the books available on Bly, Kroeger began to write her own. She discovered that the Library of Congress did not have one documented biography of Nellie Bly. There were books for young adults, most written decades before, but not a single work of scholarly research. Kroeger learned that despite Bly's hundreds of articles—all written in the first person—there was little personal information to be found. Her book, *Nellie Bly: Daredevil, Reporter, Feminist* incorporated letters and documents that Kroeger discovered and provided new insight into the reporter's life.

In the years since the book's 1994 publication, there has been renewed interest in Nellie Bly. The following year, Apollo, Pennsylvania, erected a marker in front of Bly's first home in the town. In 1997, PBS produced a documentary about Bly on its *The American Experience* program. In works of fiction, she was the focus of a 2000 episode of the television program *The West Wing*, while in 2004 author Carole Nelson Douglas incorporated Bly into her Irene Adler mystery, *Spider Dance*.

In 2002, the United States Postal Service honored Bly with her own stamp, along with stamps for Marguerite Higgins, Ethel Payne, and Ida M. Tarbell. White House correspondent Helen Thomas, who covered presidents from John F. Kennedy to Barack Obama, described the women as "unsung heroines in their time [who] displayed great courage and great integrity in uplifting the profession of journalism. They also made great contributions to America by exposing corruption, the inhumanity of social discrimination, and the horror of war."[10]

Nellie Bly worked as a reporter before cell phones, laptops, and database searches. Yet the skills she used—careful observation, vivid reporting, and insightful questions—endure.

1864 Elizabeth Jane "Pink" Cochran is born in Cochran Mills, Pennsylvania, on May 5, although later accounts will set her birth date years later.

1870 Judge Michael Cochran, Pink's father, dies without a will.

1873 Her mother, Mary Jane, marries Jack Ford, who is an abusive alcoholic.

1878 Elizabeth Jane testifies in her mother's divorce.

1879 Attends Indiana Normal School in Indiana, Pennsylvania. Lack of money forces her to leave before completing a semester.

1880 Moves to Allegheny City, near Pittsburgh, with her mother.

1885 Motivated by a column, she writes an angry letter to the *Pittsburg Dispatch*. Impressed, the editor soon gives her reporting assignments, and a new name: Nellie Bly.

1886 After writing about divorce and factory workers the year before, Bly is shunted to the women's page. She quits, leaving for Mexico, where she writes about everything from bullfighting to politics. Returning to the *Dispatch* in June, she covers the theater. Sues Colonel Samuel Jackson for mismanaging the Cochran family trust.

1887 Quits the *Dispatch*; arrives in New York City in May. After a fruitless summer, finally gets an assignment from John Cockerill at the *New York World*. Bly must pretend to be mentally ill and get committed to the asylum at Blackwell's Island. Successful in her ruse, Bly spends 10 days "in the Mad-House" before being released. Her articles are published on the front page with her name in the headline. Bly is hired as a staff reporter at the *World*.

1888   Uncovers a lobbyist who bribes assemblymen; pitches her trip around the world.

1889   On November 14, embarks on a quest to best Jules Verne's *Around the World in Eighty Days*.

1890   Bly succeeds, making her trip around the world in 72 days; she arrives on January 25. Quits the *World* to write fiction.

1893   Having failed at fiction, she returns to the *World*, covering strikes and women's rights.

1895   On April 25, Bly marries Robert Seaman, a 70-year-old millionaire.

1896   Worried that Seaman will not support her, she briefly returns to writing for the *World*. Leaves for Europe with her husband in August.

1899   Sister Kate dies. To get over her grief, Bly begins to work at her husband's company, eventually managing it and starting her own business.

1904 Robert Seaman dies. Bly runs his company, and her own—the American Steel Barrel Company, which manufactures a barrel she invented. Bly now holds 25 patents.

1910 Following the death of her company's business manager, Major Edward Gilman, Bly learns the business is heavily in debt. The company is put into bankruptcy.

1912 Bly begins to write for the *New York Evening Journal*.

1914 Travels to Austria. Later during World War I, she reports from the front lines.

1919 Returns to the United States. Her company is dissolved.

1920 Writes a column for the *Journal*; helps unwed mothers find homes for their children.

1922 Dies of bronchopneumonia on January 27. Her editor calls her "the best reporter in America."

NOTES

CHAPTER 1

1. Nellie Bly, *Around the World in Seventy-two Days*. New York: Pictorial Weeklies, 1890, p. 1. http://digital.library.upenn.edu/women/bly/world/world.html.
2. Jules Verne, *Around the World in Eighty Days*. New York: Oxford University Press, 1993, p. 17.
3. Bly, *Around the World in Seventy-two Days*, p. 3.
4. John J. Pierce, *Foundations of Science Fiction: A Study in Evolution and Imagination*. Quoted in "Jules Verne." *Authors and Artists for Young Adults*. Vol. 16. Farmington Hills, Mich.: Gale, 1995, *Gale Biography in Context*.
5. Bly, *Around the World in Seventy-two Days*, p. 2.
6. Ibid., p. 3.
7. Ibid.
8. Ibid.
9. Ibid., pp. 3–4.
10. Ibid., p. 6.
11. "A Trip Around the World," *The American Experience*, PBS.org. http://www.pbs.org/wgbh/amex/world/peopleevents/pande05.html.
12. Bly, *Around the World in Seventy-two Days*, pp. 7–8.
13. Brooke Kroeger, "Nellie Bly: She Did It All," *Quarterly of the National Archives*. Spring 1996, Vol. 28, No. 1, pp. 7–15.

CHAPTER 2

1. Brooke Kroeger, *Nellie Bly: Daredevil, Reporter, Feminist*. New York: Random House, 1994, p. 145.
2. Ibid., p. xviii.
3. Ibid., p. 14.
4. Ibid., p. 13.
5. Ibid., p. 20.

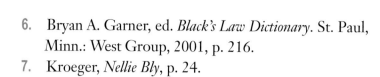

6. Bryan A. Garner, ed. *Black's Law Dictionary*. St. Paul, Minn.: West Group, 2001, p. 216.
7. Kroeger, *Nellie Bly*, p. 24.

CHAPTER 3
1. Kroeger, *Nellie Bly*, p. 34.
2. Ibid., p. 33.
3. Ibid., p. 44.
4. Ibid., p. 35.
5. Ibid., pp. 36–37.
6. Ibid., pp. 37–38.
7. Ibid., p. 35.
8. Ibid., p. 42.
9. Ibid., p. 38.
10. Ibid., p. 39.
11. Ibid., pp. 39–40.
12. Ibid., p. 40.

CHAPTER 4
1. Kroeger, *Nellie Bly*, p. 41.
2. Ibid., p. 42.
3. Ibid., p. 43.
4. Ibid., p. 44.
5. Nellie Bly, "As a White Slave." 1887 Quotidiana. Ed. Patrick Madden. July 26, 2008. http://essays. quotidiana.org/bly/white_slave/. Sept. 24, 2009.
6. Ibid.
7. Kroeger, *Nellie Bly*, pp. 47–48.
8. Ibid., p. 45.
9. Ibid.

CHAPTER 5
1. "Elizabeth Cochrane Seaman," *Encyclopedia of World Biography*, 2nd ed. 17 vols. Gale Research 1998. Re-

produced in *Biography Resource Center*. Farmington Hills, Mich. Gale, 2009. http://0-galenet.galegroup.com.millennium.newport.lib.ca.us/servlet/BioRc.

2. Kroeger, *Nellie Bly*, p. 46.

3. Ibid., p. 82.

4. Ibid., p. 49.

5. Ibid., p. 51.

6. Ibid., p. 60.

7. Nellie Bly, *Six Months in Mexico*. New York: American Publishers/N.L. Munro, 1888, pp. 21–22.

8. Ibid., p. 21.

9. Kroeger, *Nellie Bly*, p. 68.

10. Ibid., p. 65.

11. Ibid., p. 69.

12. Bly, *Six Months in Mexico*, pp. 10–11.

13. Kroeger, *Nellie Bly*, p. 69.

14. Ibid., p. 70.

15. Bly, *Six Months in Mexico*, p. 160.

16. E.A. Tweedie and Dolores Butterfield. "The Downfall of Diaz: Mexico Plunges into Revolution." 1911. *The Great Events by Famous Historians, Vol. 21*. Harrogate, Tenn.: The National Alumni, 1926. *World Book Online Reference Center*.

17. Kroeger, *Nellie Bly*, p. 69.

18. Ibid., p. 75.

19. Ibid.

CHAPTER 6

1. Thomas Kessner, *Capital City: New York City and the Men Behind America's Rise to Economic Dominance, 1860–1900*. New York: Simon & Schuster, 2003. p. 79.

2. David Ogden Stiers, "The Audacious Adventures of Nellie Bly," *The American Experience*, WGBH Educational Foundation, PBS, 1997.
3. Kroeger, *Nellie Bly*, p. 84.
4. Ibid., p. 82.
5. Ibid.
6. Ibid., p. 83.
7. Ibid., p. 85.
8. Ibid., p. 84.
9. Ibid., p. 85.
10. Nellie Bly, *Ten Days in a Mad-House*. New York: American Publishers/N.L. Munro, 1888, p. 7.
11. Ibid., p. 10.
12. Ibid.
13. Ibid., p. 26.
14. Ibid., p. 17.
15. Ibid., p. 19.
16. Ibid., p. 22.
17. Ibid., p. 24.
18. Kroeger, *Nellie Bly*, p. 91.
19. Bly, *Ten Days in a Mad-House*, p. 27.
20. Ibid.
21. Kroeger, *Nellie Bly*, p. 91.
22. Ibid., pp. 91–92.
23. Bly, *Ten Days in a Mad-House*, p. 8.
24. Ibid., p. 44.
25. Ibid., p. 63.
26. Ibid., p. 55.
27. Ibid.
28. Ibid., p. 56.
29. Ibid., p. 85.
30. Ibid., p. 69.
31. Kroeger, *Nellie Bly*, p. 94.
32. Ibid., p. 88.
33. Ibid., p. 95.

CHAPTER 7

1. "Taken Up by the Grand Jury," *New York Times*, October 20, 1887.
2. Bly, *Ten Days in a Mad-House*, p. 87.
3. Ibid., p. 88.
4. Ibid.
5. Kroeger, *Nellie Bly*, pp. 98–99.
6. Denis Brian, *Pulitzer: A Life*. New York: John Wiley & Sons, 2001, p. 127.
7. Ibid., p. 126.
8. Ibid., p. 127.
9. Kroeger, *Nellie Bly*, pp. 100–101.
10. Nellie Bly, "Trying to Be a Servant." 1887. *Quotidiana*. Ed. Patrick Madden. 24 Jun 2008. 10 Mar 2010. http://essays.quotidiana.org/bly/trying_to_be_a_servant/.
11. Ibid.
12. Ibid.
13. Ibid.
14. Ibid.
15. Ibid.
16. Nellie Bly, "As a White Slave." 1887. *Quotidiana*. Ed. Patrick Madden. 26 Jul 2008. 10 Mar 2010. http://essays.quotidiana.org/bly/white_slave/.
17. Ibid.
18. Kroeger, *Nellie Bly*, p. 105.
19. Ibid., p. 118.
20. Ibid., p. 125.
21. Brian, *Pulitzer: A Life*, p. 135.
22. Kroeger, *Nellie Bly*, p. 109.
23. Ibid., p. 113.
24. Ibid., p. 123.

CHAPTER 8

1. Bly, *Around the World in Seventy-two Days*, p. 8.

2. Ibid., p. 20.
3. Ibid., p. 23.
4. Stephen King, *On Writing*. New York: Pocket Books, 2000, p. 155.
5. Kroeger, *Nellie Bly*, p. 171.
6. Ibid., p. 149.
7. Bly, *Around the World in Seventy-two Days*, p. 32.
8. Ibid.
9. Ibid., pp. 30, 66, 84.
10. Ibid., p. 95.
11. Ibid., p. 58.
12. Kroeger, *Nellie Bly*, p. 155.
13. Bly, *Around the World in Seventy-two Days*, p. 69.
14. Ibid., pp. 76–77.
15. Ibid.
16. Ibid., p. 79.
17. Ibid., p. 87–88.
18. Ibid., pp. 89–90.
19. Ibid., pp. 96.
20. Ibid., pp. 96–97.
21. Ibid., p. 101.
22. Ibid., pp. 101–102.
23. Ibid.
24. Ibid., p. 104.
25. Ibid.
26. Kroeger, *Nellie Bly*, p. 168.

CHAPTER 9

1. Kroeger, *Nellie Bly*, p. 185.
2. Ibid., p. 187.
3. Ibid., p. 190.
4. Ibid., p. 207.
5. Ibid., p. 205.
6. Ibid., pp. 206–207.

7. Ibid., p. 209.

8. Brian, *Pulitzer: A Life*, p. 178.

9. Kroeger, *Nellie Bly*, p. 235.

10. Brian, *Pulitzer: A Life*, p. 179.

11. Ibid., pp. 186–187.

12. Kroeger, *Nellie Bly*, pp. 282–283.

13. Ibid., p. 285.

14. Ibid., p. 305.

15. Ibid., p. 327.

16. Ibid., p. 363.

CHAPTER 10

1. Kroeger, *Nellie Bly*, p. 389.

2. Ibid., p. 446.

3. Ibid., p. 407.

4. Ibid., p. 415.

5. Brooke Kroeger, "Nellie Bly: She Did It All," *Quarterly of the National Archives*. Spring 1996, Vol. 28, No. 1, p. 10.

6. Kroeger, *Nellie Bly*, p. 509.

7. "Women Come to the Front," Library of Congress, http://www.loc.gov/exhibits/wcf/wcf0002.html.

8. Barbara Ehrenreich, "Commencement Address to the University of California, Berkeley Graduate School of Journalism Class of 2009," May 16, 2009. http://www.alternet.org/story/140442/ barbara_ehrenreich:_welcome_to_a_dying_ industry,_j-school_grads/?page=entire.

9. Brian, *Pulitzer: A Life*, p. 65.

10. "Four Accomplished Journalists Honored on U.S. Postage Stamps," *Philatelic News*, September 14, 2002. http://www.usps.com/news/2002/philatelic/ sr02_063.html.

BIBLIOGRAPHY

BOOKS

Baxandall, Rosalyn, and Linda Gordon, eds. *America's Working Women: A Documentary History, 1600 to the Present.* New York: W.W. Norton, 1995.

Blondheim, Manahem. *News over the Wires: The Telegraph and the Flow of Public Information in America, 1844–1897.* Cambridge, Mass.: Harvard University Press, 1994.

Bly, Nellie. *Around the World in Seventy-two Days.* New York: Pictorial Weeklies, 1890.

———. *Six Months in Mexico.* New York: American Publishers/N.L. Munro, 1888.

———. *Ten Days in a Mad-House.* New York: American Publishers/N.L. Munro, 1888.

Brian, Denis. *Pulitzer: A Life.* New York: John Wiley & Sons, 2001.

Buk-Swienty, Tom. *The Other Half: The Life of Jacob Riis and the World of Immigrant America.* New York: W.W. Norton, 2008.

Kessner, Thomas. *Capital City: New York City and the Men Behind America's Rise to Economic Dominance, 1860–1900.* New York: Simon & Schuster, 2003.

Kroeger, Brooke. *Nellie Bly: Daredevil, Reporter, Feminist.* New York: Random House, 1994.

Moorehead, Caroline. *Gellhorn: A Twentieth-Century Life.* New York: Henry Holt, 2003.

Thomas, Helen. *Watchdogs of Democracy?* New York: Scribner, 2006.

PERIODICALS

Kroeger, Brooke. "Nellie Bly: She Did It All," *Quarterly of the National Archives.* Spring 1996, Vol. 28, No. 1.

Lowry, Patricia. "Bessie Bramble: A Force for Change,"
    Pittsburgh Post-Gazette. March 4, 2007. Available online.
    URL: http://www.post-gazette.com/pg/07063/766082-
    51.stm.

"Taken up by the Grand Jury," *New York Times*. Octo-
    ber 20, 1887, p. 2.

OTHER SOURCES

Contemporary Authors Online, Gale, 2010. Reproduced
    in *Biography Resource Center*. Farmington Hills, Mich.:
    Gale, 2010.

Dictionary of American Biography Base Set. American
    Council of Learned Societies, 1928–1936. Reproduced
    in *Biography Resource Center*. Farmington Hills, Mich.:
    Gale, 2010.

"Jane Croly." *Encyclopedia of World Biography Supplement*,
    Vol. 21. Gale Group, 2001. Reproduced in *Biography
    Resource Center*. Farmington Hills, Mich.: Gale, 2010.

"Stephen Collins Foster." *Encyclopedia of World Biogra-
    phy*, 2nd ed. 17 Vols. Gale Research, 1998. Reproduced
    in *Biography Resource Center*. Farmington Hills, Mich.:
    Gale, 2010.

DVD

"The Audacious Adventures of Nellie Bly," *The American
    Experience*, WGBH Educational Foundation, PBS. 1997.

WEB SITES

"American Experience: Nellie Bly," PBS.org. Available
    online. URL: http://www.pbs.org/wgbh/amex/world/
    peopleevents/pande01.html.

"Apollo Area Historical Society," Armstrong History. Available online. URL: http://www.armstronghistory.org/apollo/.

"The Battle of the Wilderness," Shotgun's Home of the American Civil War. Available online. URL: http://civilwarhome.com/wildernessor.htm.

"The Borough of Apollo, Pennsylvania," Available online. URL: http://www.apollopa.org/.

"Brooke Kroeger's Nellie Bly," New York Correction History Society Web site. Available online. URL: http://www.correctionhistory.org/rooseveltisland/bly.

"Elizabeth Shepley Sergeant," Spartacus Educational. Available online. URL: http://www.spartacus.schoolnet.co.uk/FWWsergeant.htm.

"History of Public Transportation in New York City," New York Transit Museum. Available online. URL: http://www.transitmuseumeducation.org/trc/background.

"Indiana Normal School Board of Trustees," Indiana University of Pennsylvania Web site. Available online. URL: http://www.iup.edu/page.aspx?id=86177.

"Nellie Bly 1864–1922." Available online. URL: http://www.library.csi.cuny.edu/dept/history/lavender/386/nellie.html.

"People and Events: Ida Tarbell, 1857–1944," American Experience: The Rockefellers. Available online. URL: http://www.pbs.org/wgbh/amex/rockefellers/peopleevents/p_tarbell.html.

"Quick Stats on Women Workers, 2009," U.S. Department of Labor. Available online. URL: http://www.dol.gov/wb/stats/main.htm.

Sheffield, Gary. "The Origins of World War One." BBC History, March 8, 2011. Available online. URL: http://www.bbc.co.uk/history/worldwars/wwone/origins_01.shtml.

"Sob Sisters: The Image of the Female Journalist in Popular Culture," Image of the Journalist in Popular Culture, January 2011. Available online. URL: http://www.ijpc.org/sobsmaster.htm.

"Welcome to a Dying Industry, J-School Grads," AlterNet, June 4, 2009. Available online. URL: http://www.alternet.org/story/140442/barbara_ehrenreich:_welcome_to_a_dying_industry,_j-school_grads/?page=entire.

"Women Journalists and Editors," About.com. Available online. URL: http://womenshistory.about.com/od/journalists/Women_Journalists_and_Editors.htm.

"Women's Issues Then & Now: A Feminist Overview of the Past Two Centuries." Available online. URL: http://www.cwrl.utexas.edu/~ulrich/femhist/marriage.shtml.

FURTHER RESOURCES

BOOKS

Chambers, Deborah, Linda Steiner, and Carole Fleming. *Women and Journalism*. New York: Routledge, 2004.

Macy, Sue. *Bylines: A Photobiography of Nellie Bly*. Washington, D.C.: National Geographic Society, 2008.

Whitt, Jan. *Women in American Journalism: A New History*. Urbana: University of Illinois Press, 2008.

WEB SITES

National Women's History Museum: Women With a Deadline
http://www.nwhm.org/online-exhibits/ womenwithdeadlines/wwd1.htm

Nellie Bly 1864–1922
http://www.library.csi.cuny.edu/dept/history/ lavender/386/nellie.html

Women Come to the Front: Journalists, Photographers, and Broadcasters during World War II
http://www.loc.gov/exhibits/wcf/

PICTURE CREDITS

Page

INDEX

ABOUT THE AUTHOR

Born in Boston, Massachusetts, JOHN BANKSTON began writing professionally while still a teenager. Since then, more than 200 of his articles have been published in magazines and newspapers across the country, including the *Tallahassee Democrat*, the *Orlando Sentinel*, and the *Ocala-Star Banner*. He also worked as an investigative reporter for the *Tallahassean*. He is the author of more than 60 biographies for young adults, including works on scientist Stephen Hawking, anthropologist Margaret Mead, author F. Scott Fitzgerald, and actor Heath Ledger. He currently lives on Balboa Island in Newport Beach, California.

219
⑥